Informal Education - conversation, democracy and learning

First published 1996.
Second edition, revised and updated: 1999.
Reprinted 2001.
Third edition, revised and updated: 2005

Educational Heretics Press 113 Arundel Drive, Bramcote, Nottingham NG9 3FQ

British Cataloguing in Publication Data

A catalogue record for this book is available from the British Library

ISBN 1-900219-29-8

Set in Book Antiqua and Gill Sans

Cover design by John Haxby

Printed by NPM, Riverside Road, Pride Park
Derby DE24 8HA

Contents

2   Informal Education

Acknowledgements

Many people - students, colleagues and friends have provided feedback on the earlier editions of this book. We are grateful for their help and guidance. In particular Michele Erina Doyle and Ruth Gilchrist supplied detailed suggestions regarding ways in which the first edition might be improved. These were incorporated in the second edition. Michele also made suggestions for this edition. To them we owe a special debt of gratitude.

Thanks are also due to the Rank Foundation for helping fund the Foundation Studies in Informal and Community Education programme for which parts of this book were initially prepared.

Introduction

When we talk of education we tend to focus on what happens in schools and colleges. Yet so much of our learning takes place beyond classrooms and outside courses. Each and every day, many of us set out to create opportunities for learning. We may do this for ourselves, for example, through reading a book or watching television. We are also involved in learning with others - at work, at home and in the various social groups to which we belong. Processes such as these are the 'bread and butter' of informal educators.

Informal educators at work

We can think about informal education as the 'teaching' that goes on in daily life. As friends, for example, we may well encourage others to talk about things that have happened in their lives so that they can handle their feelings and to think about what to do next. As parents or carers we may show children how to write different words or tie their shoe laces. As situations arise we respond.

Others may view informal education as the learning projects that we undertake for ourselves. We may take up astronomy, for example, and then start reading around the subject, buying magazines and searching out other people interested in the area. This is often, better, described as 'self-education'.

Many view informal education as the learning that flows from the conversations and activities involved in being members of youth and community groups and the like. In these settings there are workers whose job it is to encourage people to think about experiences and situations. Like friends or parents they may respond to what is going on but, as 'specialists', these workers are able to bring different insights and ways of working and being. This book has been written mainly for this group of workers. It explores how they can encourage deeper and more reflective conversations, pick up on questions that need exploring, and help people to lead happier and more fulfilled lives. In doing this they engage in many of the same activities as parents, carers and friends – but because they may have more space to respond, and may draw upon different resources and ways of thinking they are able to give things a 'twist'. When we use the term 'informal educator' in this book it generally refers to those who consciously take up this role and challenge.

Like other educators, these informal educators are teachers – they foster environments for learning. However, where they do this, and how they do this, can set them apart. Many play, youth, community and adult and community education workers may see informal education as the core of their work. Others, such as nurses, caseworkers, schoolteachers and police officers, may view it as an aspect of their activities. Titles and settings, however, can be misleading. Not everything that takes place in a youth project or play centre is informal education, just as a good part of schooling is not formal education. We hope what follows will help people to distinguish between the two.

Informal educators work in a multitude of ways. They exploit and create learning opportunities. We can find them building relationships through sport, the arts, social activities, the provision of welfare services, and regular contact. The fostering of conversation - working so that people can engage with, and learn from, each other and the world – is central to their work. However, much of their influence flows from the people they are. They are listened to and their example is followed because they have gained people's respect.

These informal educators have to run with the issues and interests that people bring with them. They have to 'go with the flow'. As a result there can be no simple 'how to' formula. Like all educators they improvise, but more so. This makes the work rewarding but difficult and challenging. Informal educators have to think for themselves, they cannot follow some pre-set curriculum or plan. The immediate aims may change from situation to situation. At one point they may be seeking to promote healthy eating, at another helping someone to explore their feelings and relationships. Yet there is a larger purpose - fostering democracy and enabling people to live a life worth living.

These informal educators also work where people are. That means they have to learn to operate in a range of settings. Often they are visitors – entering environments over which they have little or no control such as shopping centres, schools, health centres and people's homes. Sometimes they have to find ways of attracting people to join them. They may organize festivals or run groups. Their work is always influenced by the 'where'. Educators have to be sensitive to the setting – what may be appropriate for one may not be for another. As a result, they need to think carefully about their language and demeanour. What works in a hospital may not on the street.

Last, but not least, informal education is not tied to an age or client group. For example, we find informal educators working with children, young people, those in residential care, adults on local housing estates, carers, students and religious groups.

All this means that to be successful educators must be interested in other people and the world, and be interesting in themselves. They have to bring wisdom to their relationships; try to live their lives as well as they can; and always be open to learning. Also they need to embody some special qualities. People must want to have contact with them, to share time with them. As such they must be warm, engaging and aware. Simply being 'around' is never enough.

Informal learning, self-education and incidental learning

Much learning takes place without being consciously organised. Such learning is sometimes referred to as 'informal learning'. We take things on board during the course of our daily activities - usually by doing tasks, observing or talking to others. Our learning in these cases is rarely intentional in any narrow sense, it simply occurs. For example, our vocabulary is enriched via casual reading, listening and talking; our practical and social skills improve because we watch and absorb what we see. The more alert and inquisitive we are the more we learn; the more self-absorbed and uncritical, the less likely we are to learn. The greater our interest in other people and the world around us the more will be taught by them and it. As a result such 'informal learning' is not purely a matter of good fortune. It, like chance, as the scientist Louise Pasteur explained 'favours the prepared mind'.

Trying to understand what is involved in 'informal learning' and how it works is difficult. Much discussion of it is 'ill-defined' and the processes involved 'messy'[1]. Sometimes people use 'informal learning' when they mean self-education. The latter involves a deliberate effort to learn and often some planning. Self-educators take themselves to places where they expect learning will occur. For example, they assume a visit to an art gallery will enable them to better understand paintings, or a horse show riding. Self-educators seek out books or people whom they judge will aid their learning. They embark on an educational journey. It is not necessarily an isolated passage. Self-educators enter into 'conversations' with others such as the writers of the books they study, the curators of museums they visit, and with those they observe and converse with.

Self-education and informal education are closely related. First, the informal educators we are concerned with seek to promote self-education, to encourage others to 'take charge of their own education'. Second, these educators consciously make themselves a resource for those engaged in self-education. They make themselves available as a friend and

---

[1] Elizabeth Sommerlad (1999) *Informal Learning and Widening Participation*. London: The Tavistock Institute.

tutor willing to counsel, encourage and sustain those who have embarked on a journey of self-education.

As we have seen, sometimes people use 'informal learning' when they mean incidental learning or what Alan Rogers has called acquisition learning (see page 15). Such learning happens as part of doing something else. We are aware of the task but not necessarily the learning involved. This is also an area of great interest to informal educators like youth workers and community educators. They foster environments conducive to such learning. They get people involved in activities and tasks - and the learning involved is often not overt nor is it necessarily predictable. They also often try to stimulate interest directly in different issues and questions. For example, workers based in a community centre might use posters, sponsor outings to places of interest or invite stimulating visitors to drop-in. Again, what may be learnt is often not what was intended and frequently not as the result of direct intervention by the workers.

Many informal educators we meet know learning like this can be exhilarating - especially when it enables people to make connections and look afresh at what they took for granted. They know how it can enrich lives and how observing or overhearing a nearby conversation can both teach us something 'we never knew before' and brighten up a tedious bus journey, or long wait for a friend. Because informal educators aim to advance learning and open it up to as many people as possible they naturally seek to build upon such incidental learning. They use it as a starting point, and try to deepen learning through encouraging conversation, reflection and further experience. In other words, informal educators both consciously set out to create environments that foster incidental learning, and encourage people to explore what may have been learnt.

The tradition of informal education

Obviously informal education is not a new practice. Long before mass schooling, teachers and taught worked together in everyday settings. It was a part of family, work and social life. Ideas were shared, skills developed and values tested. The work of 'specialist' informal educators today has inherited such ways of working and has adapted many of the old settings. Youth groups, community groups and study circles, for example, are part of a long tradition of voluntary and largely self-organized education.

Despite having a long and distinguished history, some we meet at work and elsewhere are unsure what 'informal education' is. Not a few, we suspect, view it as the new-fangled brainchild of some policy-maker or academic. This is partly understandable for the term only really became widely known in Britain around half a century ago with the publication of a remarkable book *Informal Education*. The book was written by Josephine Macalister Brew[2], who then worked for the National Association of Girls' and Mixed Clubs. It looked at how educational opportunities might be developed and sustained 'beyond the classroom' in clubs, community associations and almost anywhere where people congregate. As such informal education may be seen as part of a tradition of education dating back over 2500 years.

For a long time dialogue and conversation have been viewed by many as the natural way to wisdom and understanding for adults. In Ancient Greece, for example, instruction and the classroom were places reserved for those not seen as mature enough to join in. It was assumed free citizens would best learn from each other via dialogue and discourse. They gathered in the Forum and on the streets to talk, debate and test each other's ideas. In more recent times clubs, debating societies, coffee-houses, reading groups, community centres, youth clubs and the internet have carried on in this tradition. Such open, and often self-organized, education has survived wars, suppression and attempt by governments to channel education towards the narrowly vocational and pre-packaged learning. It is no accident that informal educators seek to foster democracy and promote conversation that entails the pursuit of truth.

---

[2] Josephine Macalister Brew (1946) *Informal Education: Adventures and Reflections*. London: Faber and Faber.

They do so because that is, in significant part, the tradition from which they have emerged.

Here we can see something of the challenge and promise of informal education. It is the process of fostering learning in life as it is lived. A concern with community and conversation; a focus on people as persons rather than objects; a readiness to educate in different settings - these offer the possibility of seeing work in new ways. It may also help explain why, for many, informal education is more than a job. It is a calling, something that demands commitment.[3]

Follow up

The introduction has tried to put this book into a context; to explain where we, as the writers, 'come from' and where the book is heading. It will be helpful to read other books and articles alongside this. First, it may help you understand better what we are saying. Second, and more importantly, doing so should make it easier for you, the reader, to embark on a dialogue with us: to talk back at the page rather than accept it. The texts identified at the end of every chapter often offer a different take. Some adopt a radically different stance.

Read Josephine Macalister Brew's (1946) *Informal Education. Adventures and reflections*, London: Faber and Faber. This book is a wonderful starting point for those who wish to sit alongside a practitioner who thinks deeply about her work and endeavours to make better sense of what she does. It is well worth reading from cover to cover. However, it can now only be bought second-hand or borrowed from a library.

Read Clive Erricker (2002) *When Learning Becomes Your Enemy*, Nottingham: Educational Heretics Press. We are so

---

[3]   Michele Erina Doyle (1999) 'Called to be an informal educator', *Youth and Policy* 65. Available via our web support.

trained to view education as something that belongs in and, usually, takes place within schools and colleges that it often seems incomprehensible anyone would question their value. However it is important to ponder the work of writers who seriously probe our common-sense assumptions and find them wanting. Writers and practitioners who value education but are sceptical about the worth of 'formal' education often have deep sympathy for informal approaches. Erricker's book challenges much orthodox thinking about education. A highly regarded alternative is Ivan Illich (1971) *Deschooling Society*. Harmondsworth: Penguin.

Read Tony Jeffs 'The history of informal education' in Linda Deer Richardson and Mary Wolfe (eds.) (2001) *The Principles and Practice of Informal Education*, London: RoutledgeFalmer. This piece provides an introduction to the development of informal education as a practice.

Visit the *Informal Education* support page at www.infed.org/foundations for further discussion, examples, activities and links. You can find more on the ideas discussed here – and pieces on Brew and Illich.

Chapter 1

Being an informal educator

There is a wonderful scene in one of George Eliot's books. Her central character, Felix Holt, is talking with Rufus Lyon, a deacon in a local chapel.

> Felix rose to go, and said, "I will not take up more of your valuable time, Mr. Lyon. I know that you have not many spare evenings."
>
> "That is true, my young friend; for I now go to Sproxton one evening in the week. I do not despair that we may some day need a chapel there, though the hearers do not multiply save among the women, and there is no work as yet begun among the miners themselves..."
>
> "O, I've been to Sproxton already several times. I had a congregation of my own there last Sunday evening."
>
> "What! do you preach?" said my Lyon, with a brightened glance.
>
> "Not exactly. I went to the ale-house"
>
> Mr. Lyon started. "I trust you are putting a riddle to me, young man, even as Samson did to his companions. From what you said but lately, it cannot be that you are given over to tippling and to taverns."
>
> "O, I don't drink much. I order a pint of beer, and I get into talk with the fellows over their pots and pipes. Somebody must take a little knowledge and

common sense to them in this way, else how are they to get it? I go for educating the non-electors, so I put myself in the way of my pupils - my academy is the beer-house." [4]

Many people, like Rufus Lyon, link process with place: preaching with chapels, educating with schools and so on. The images we mostly have of educators are of chalk and talk; of classrooms, rows of desks, lessons, exams, battles for order, punishments. Felix Holt, chatting over a pint of beer, is not what many expect. Yet this is a good example of informal education. Holt:

- Joins in with an activity (puts himself 'in the way of his pupils').

- Uses an everyday setting where people have chosen to be.

- Engages people in conversation.

- Seeks to foster learning.

The focus for learning is given by the full title of Eliot's novel - *Felix Holt, the Radical*. Holt is committed to political change, to the advancement of the working class. He wants to see changes to a world 'that is not a very fine place for a good many people in it'. This mix of commitment and participation often marks out informal educators. To get a better grip on such qualities we need to look at learning in familiar or everyday settings. This involves examining how we use thought, understanding, memory and a range of approaches to educating.

Learning

There is a phrase 'you are learning all the time'. Certainly we are thinking all the time. To go about our lives we have to make sense of the world around us. Just walking down the

---

[4]   George Eliot (1866) *Felix Holt, The Radical*, London: Dent, pages 66-7. The second quotation is from page 57.

road, for example, involves thought - being on the look-out for holes in the path and so on. For the most part we are not aware of such matters. We often become alive to what is going on in our minds when something is not 'right' or is unusual. For example, each day we may walk past a tree without 'seeing it'. This morning it isn't there - and with a jolt we notice. We start wondering - where is it? John Dewey, the American educator, had a phrase for this moment. He said that thinking begins in what might be called a 'forked-road situation that is ambiguous, that presents a dilemma, that proposes alternatives'[5]. In our view, it is not so much thinking that begins here as our awareness of it.

Much of the learning we engage in is related to a particular task. We may be conscious of the task, but not of the learning involved. Here, we only have to think about all the tasks involved in parenting to see how this might happen. Alan Rogers has helpfully described this as 'acquisition learning' and contrasted it with 'learning-conscious' or formalized learning[6]. In the latter people are aware that the task they are engaged in involves learning. Much of what we do as informal educators is concerned with creating an environment where 'acquisition learning' can take place. However, we also often seek to create a 'forked road', to encourage people to explore what is going on. We do this by asking questions and engaging in conversations that challenge the 'accepted'. We may also create events or change environments e.g. altering the layout of a room to stimulate surprise and exploration. This is done not only to entertain or to amuse. It is also to help people consciously think, understand and learn from, and about, their world.

To think, we have to remember. Again this is going on all the time without our being especially aware of it. In many

---

5   John Dewey (1933) *How We Think*, New York: D. C. Heath, page 212.

6   Alan Rogers (2003) *What is the Difference? A new critique of adult learning and teaching*, Leicester: NIACE.

respects it cannot be set aside from thinking. To remember we have to think about the past. A certain smell, a song may start us off. We summon up images, evoke feelings, grab at snatches of conversation. Memories are, thus, not things we simply take off the shelf, dust down and display. They have to be conjured up - thought about. This process of remaking the past explains why our memory of a thing or event changes.

How we are feeling when we think about the past also influences the way we remember things. The process of making memory - and the way it is wrapped up in our moods - means that we should take care not to take remembering for granted. In other words, sometimes we need to think about how we are thinking when looking back. So it is that informal educators often seek to stimulate memories. Through dialogue about the past we may help people better understand themselves, the situations they encounter and what they can do.

In this way people can find understanding - what psychologists often call comprehension. One way of thinking about understanding is that it is the opposite of confusion[7]. If we are able to make sense of what is going on we 'understand'. This is not a passive thing, but an active process. As Frank Smith put it, understanding - meaningfulness - has to be imposed on the world. We have to name things to make sense. Thus, educators name certain actions for a purpose. We can name words used unthinkingly in conversation by others as 'racist', for example. From this action understanding may grow.

Understanding is not simply a matter of knowing things. We can sometimes know about something without actually understanding it. For example, we might know about what is happening in a famine - but we may not understand it. When we say we 'understand' something we are saying that we can place various parts of the problem in relation to one another. And here we can see our role as informal educators coming into play. In conversation we may introduce new

---

[7]   Frank Smith (1992) *To Think*, London: Routledge, page 35.

perspectives, for example, around North/South inequalities. In so doing ideas can be linked together and explored.

Now we can turn to learning. We can initially approach learning as a product or thing. When we say we have learnt something what we usually mean is that we have gained some understanding that we have been able to commit to memory. We call the memory 'learning'. We have learnt this or that. Frank Smith describes this as seeking to stamp a seal of approval on particular thoughts and feelings that we want to stay with us in the future. For example, we may be trying to learn French. We may read words and then repeat them to ourselves hoping we can capture them and hold them so we can use them again.

We can also approach learning as a process that we all engage in. Like memorization and understanding, it involves thinking. In other words, learning isn't simply a memory that we label as knowledge; it is also the way we search for understanding. It is something that we do. For much of the time, easy and unseen, learning is thinking that takes us forward. It prepares us for what might be. Thus, as Frank Smith has put it, remembering involves the past, understanding the present; and learning is oriented to the future. Each of these words describes thinking - but emphasizes different aspects.

Education

Now we may think about education. Education is concerned with all aspects of thinking. However, it is future-oriented - it is about development and growth, even when we are studying the past. Thus, as educators, the aspect of thinking we tend to focus upon is learning. As we have stressed, much thinking is commonplace - it goes on all the time, often without our being aware of it. Education takes us into the conscious world. It involves activities that are intended to stimulate thinking, to foster learning. We set out to help another person to learn, or to learn something ourselves (a process of self-education). Both can take place at the same time. We learn as we teach. In conversation we learn about people and communities and also learn the craft of informal education.

Intention

Sometimes, such as when teaching in a classroom, we may have a detailed idea about what we are trying to achieve. We might even have written down a lesson plan with some objectives. We may have a script and a syllabus - we know there are certain things about which we need to talk and things we wish to teach. However, a lot of the time we may not have such a clear idea of where things are headed. All we have is a picture of the general direction that we want to go in. Sitting in with a group of people as they watch a soap opera in a hostel, for example, we will be talking a lot less (if we know what is good for us!). There will be some conversation - perhaps arising from the plot. We will usually have no idea as to what is coming and how people will react. One of the characters in the programme might be thinking about having an abortion. This could produce a discussion on the rights of fathers, a diatribe against the Pope or a venomous attack on single mothers. Who knows?

Conversation is unpredictable. Things are said - hopefully people listen and work with the ideas - developing them, shaping them. As we listen we begin to understand that it may be educationally helpful for it to go in this direction or that. But we could not know that this is where we would go before the conversation started. As educators we have joined in with the aim of fostering learning - but we are not able to specify the subject matter to the same extent as the classroom teacher. Indeed, our concern for conversation and democracy mean we should not set limits on what might be discussed, or what others should learn. However, this openness may create difficulties. While the subject matter is open, our commitments demand we attend to the way things are approached. We need to focus on the content and the process, and explore with people how these relate to core values such as respect for persons. This involves respecting individuals' rights to determine what is to be talked about and the rights of others not to be silenced or demeaned.

Environment

John Dewey made the point that we are not able to plug directly into another person's brain. 'We never educate directly, but indirectly by means of the environment'. He continued, 'Whether we permit chance environments to do the work, or whether we design environments for the purpose makes a great difference'.[8] If we think of environment in the way that say Greenpeace might use the term then what we are focusing on is a physical thing. It is the world around us. We, thus, look at the state of the air, the quality of our rivers, the shape of our towns and villages. A substitute word is 'surrounding'.

But the word can also be used in another way - such as when we talk about the environment of a group. Here the focus is on the relationships between people rather than physical or material conditions. Individuals participate in some activity - be it talking, watching a video or making some thing. The process we go through has meaning for each of us involved. We attach value to, and think and feel about, it in various ways. Through our interactions we create social, and hence emotional and political, environments.

To appreciate situations we need to attend to both aspects for they are two sides of the same coin. The physical environment - the shape of the room, the way chairs are laid out, lighting and heating will influence the way we feel and think about the activities we are engaged in. In turn, our social relationships will affect the way we view these things. We will often, in the course of our work, deliberately change the environment to cater for different groups - to attract some or drive out others. This we may do in various ways - the music played, the activities available and so on.

---

[8]   John Dewey (1916) *Democracy and Education*, New York: Macmillan, page 16.

Commitment

So far we have seen that education involves us in setting out to foster environments that make for learning. However, we can't leave it there. It is not learning for learning sake. Nurses, when acting as informal educators, seek to enhance the life chances of those they encounter. We do not act as educators in a value free way. We carry with us ideas about what makes for human well-being. Health educators will have an idea as to what is a healthy lifestyle. Their conversation will be influenced by this - some behaviours may be encouraged, others not.

Some, it must be recognized, will employ informal techniques to put forward racist ideas, encourage homophobia and highly suspect notions such as 'family values'. This is not unusual, youth workers in projects, teachers in classrooms, doctors in surgeries and police officers in the station may well express such views. But can this be seen as 'education'? We believe not.

In our view, for something to be called 'education', whether it takes place in the classroom or the canteen, it must be informed by certain values (we discuss these in Chapter 7). There is a dividing line between education and indoctrination. Education, unlike the latter, embraces a commitment to:

- Respect for persons.

- The promotion of well-being.

- Truth.

- Democracy.

- Fairness and equality.

It is also an intensely hopeful activity. For us education is founded on the belief that things can be improved, that people can change. We have to have an idea of what is possible and a belief that we can make some difference. This involves us looking for, and building up, the good in others (and ourselves)[9].

These values and this orientation should inform both the content of conversations, as well as our behaviour and relationships as educators. Julius Nyerere once summed these concerns up when he talked of the purpose of education as being the liberation of humans from the restraints and limitations of ignorance and dependency. 'Nothing else can be properly called education. Teaching which induces a slave mentality or a sense of impotence is not education at all - it is an attack on the minds of men'.[10]

In recent years some workers have described such concerns in terms of a commitment to the empowerment of 'clients'. They may argue that their task is not to train people to 'fit in' but to work with them to secure power. At one level this may be laudable, at another it can be patronizing, even dishonest. First, we argue that as educators we strive so that all may share in a common life. Part of our task may, thus, be to work with people so that they do 'fit in', that they become part of a community. Second, problems arise when we talk of empowering others. This implies that as educators we give power to people. We make them powerful or able. This position is neither possible nor desirable. As educators we work with others to create environments for learning. We don't change people, people change themselves in interaction with others. To talk of empowering people is, thus, to risk being anti-liberatory. At worst it encourages dependency of the 'empowered' on the 'empowerer' and a view of people as objects to be acted upon. It can also obscure the nature of the processes actually involved. Power is a feature of relationships. It is not something given or gifted.

---

9   See David Halpin (2003) *Hope and Education. The role of the utopian imagination*, London: Routledge Falmer.

10   Julius K. Nyerere (1978) 'Development is for Man, by Man, and of Man', in B. L. Hall and J. R. Kidd (eds) *Adult Learning: A design for action*, Oxford: Pergamon, pp. 27-8.

Informal and formal education

For years informal educators have been encouraged to define themselves by saying what they are not. And in the main what they are not are schoolteachers. In conversation a series of opposites often emerge. Informal educators supposedly offer choice not compulsion; freedom not order; 'empowerment' not indoctrination. As we have seen, things are not so simple. Educators in formal and informal settings, we believe, have far more in common than both often admit.

If we return to Dewey's definition then we can say that both informal and formal educators have to pay attention to the environment. However, more formal approaches involve educators attempting to manage the environment (physical and social) in a way that is not possible for informal educators. After all, teachers run schools, they decide who is in which class, what lessons will take place when, and the rules that all must obey if they wish to avoid punishment. Informal educators are rarely in the same position. There is also something more here. Formal educators set out with a much tighter idea about what is to be achieved.

Let us compare schoolteachers with street or detached youth workers. For much of the time schoolteachers are able to exert some degree of control over physical setting, for example, they can lay out the classroom in a certain way. Street workers cannot do this. They have to operate for much of the time within social settings such as the shopping mall, or village square. They can't control the physical environment in the same way. What they can do is try to choose places that might make for a convivial setting for learning. They might encourage people to go to a particular cafe or corner (that is quieter).

Schoolteachers are also able to work on the social environment (although there is often resistance to this by students). They try to control exchanges between students. They set work, design activities and so on. Street workers rely on conversation, and what is happening around them. Not surprisingly, one street worker claimed the essential skill required for such work was, 'learning to listen to many conversations at the same time in order to know which one to join in with'.

Last, schoolteachers, for a lot of the time, are working from a syllabus or a curriculum that sets out what they should be teaching - and provides for some basic form of evaluation. They, or increasingly their employers, have a great deal of control over content. Street workers do not. They depend on the twists and turns of conversation. Yes, they may introduce some subject, they may even do battle to keep the subject in front of people, but often they are fighting a lost cause. They have to go with the flow.

Informal education is based around conversation, formal around curriculum. Informal educators cannot design environments, nor direct proceedings in quite the same way as formal educators. As John Dewey says this does make a difference. But we should not say one is better than the other - they are simply not the same. We may work informally in one situation, formally in another. How we approach matters would depend on what is involved and appropriate.

By setting informal against formal education we run the risk of not seeing the shared concern for learning. We can approach them as unconnected, but that is mistaken. First, good schoolteachers, like good informal educators, desire to help people grow and learn so all may share in a common life. They seek to educate not indoctrinate.

Second, informal educators will at times adopt formal methods. They may teach around a curriculum, organize and manage groups and activities. Equally, teachers may have their informal times as well as their formal ones. An example from schooling may help. A senior school was having problems of bullying and vandalism during break times. Previously, students were not allowed in the building. The staff decided to try an 'informal education approach', although they did not call it such. All students could stay inside. A 'tuck shop' was opened, and several rooms became social areas. However, the key change involved teachers spending time with young people during break times. They saw their role less as policing and more as developing relationships, engaging in conversation. The corridors came to resemble shopping malls with groups of students promenading and others sitting, talking and looking on.

Some remain in the classrooms working. Bullying declined until it almost ceased to be a problem.

It is best to see informal and formal education as a continuum. John Ellis has drawn a diagram that expresses this.

Figure 1.1: The informal/formal education continuum[11]

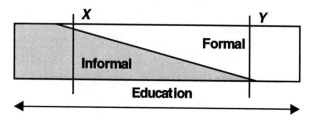

If we look at this then the street workers probably work more towards X; schoolteachers toward Y. That means both engage in a mixture of formal and informal practice. Put another way - both have to be facilitators, both have to be teachers. Each will attend to process, and have a range of outcomes in mind. Both will find it difficult to assess success if they are concerned with more than the gaining of specific knowledge and skills. They have to learn to trust - trust in their judgement and their own assessment of what does and does not constitute learning.

In conclusion

So when we ask the question 'what is it to be an informal educator?' - the answer is that it means, first and foremost, being an educator. This involves seeking to foster learning in the situations where we work. It entails cultivating environments in which people are able to remember significant experiences, and to work at understanding them.

---

11 Developed from John Ellis (1990) 'Informal education - a Christian perspective' in Tony Jeffs and Mark K. Smith (eds.) *Using Informal Education*, Buckingham: Open University Press.

It also means creating situations where people can experience new things.

Those working in everyday social situations need to define themselves primarily by conversation. They may at times use formal settings and have a curriculum to follow, but the balance of their work names them as informal educators. By becoming part of the familiar and everyday, educators can embed relationships, values and ways of being with each other, that foster understanding, democracy and learning. This is the promise of informal education.

Some questions to consider

1. Education involves setting out with the intention of fostering learning. It entails influencing the environment; and is based on a commitment to certain values such as a respect for persons. Think about your work with people - are these things that you look to?

2. We can separate informal from formal education using the amount of control over the environment; and the way the educational encounter is 'planned'. What control do you have over the environments in which you work? Are your work encounters with people planned?

3. What mix of informal and formal education do you use? Where do you stand between X and Y in *Figure 1.1*?

4. Education involves facilitating and teaching. How do you feel about describing yourself as a facilitator or teacher?

5. Are there any subjects or issues that informal educators should not discuss or raise?

Follow up

There are several things you can do to deepen your exploration of being an informal educator.

Visit the 'being an informal educator' support page at www.infed.org/foundations for further discussion, examples, activities and links.

Read 'For those who need to be learners', Chapter 1 of Eduard Lindeman's classic 1926 book: *The Meaning of Adult Education*, Norman, Oklahoma: Oklahoma Research Centre for Continuing Professional and Higher Education. Lindeman sets out the elements of an education that honours life. You can find an extract and more about Lindeman on the support page.

Read Carl Rogers on 'The interpersonal relationship in the facilitation of learning' in H. Kirschenbaum and V. L. Henderson (eds.) (1990) *The Carl Rogers Reader*, London: Constable pages 304-322. [A version can also be found in his book with H. J. Freiberg (1994) *Freedom to Learn*, New York: Merrill.] Rogers' focus on relationship and being is still fresh and inspiring to many who read it. You can find out more about Carl Rogers on the support page.

Chapter 2

Trusting in conversation

Conversation is central to our work as informal educators, yet we often undervalue it. Some of us may be uncomfortable 'just sitting around talking'. We may feel we ought to be *doing* something such as running an 'activity'. Others may get frustrated by the 'trivial' nature of everyday talk - last night's television, what X said to Y. Yet the seemingly banal can be quite something else. It can have hidden depths. Here we want to explore the nature and power of talk; and how trusting in conversation can carry us forward.

Talking with others

There is something very special about talking with others. We can see it in common phrases such as 'I have just got to get this off my chest' or 'if I don't tell someone I will burst'. We use and hear words like these when we are upset or have experienced something that has affected us deeply. We can often feel a great need to share things with others, to tell someone. The act of talking, of trying to put these feelings into words can be a help in itself. This isn't simply because we have been able to name an emotion, to speak our thoughts out loud - but because someone else is there with us, involved in our efforts. We are sharing our concerns and interests.

We can also see the same process at work in situations where there is no dramatic news or problem to be shared. Here we need only reflect on our own experiences, for example, when we have been 'cooped up' in the house or apartment all day with nobody to talk to. We may welcome having time to ourselves, but at some point it is liable to pall. We may phone a friend, or go to the local cafe or to a place where we know we will meet people. The talk we then engage in may seem fairly trivial - the everyday things of life - but that contact, that chance to interact, to be with others is affirming. We are a human with other humans. We are addressing each other.

One of the of the most inhumane of all punishments is solitary confinement. Depriving people of contact with others can lead to breakdown. Similarly, groups may exclude members as a punishment for 'breaking the rules' or for being different. Informal educators are often challenged by such behaviour. It is tempting to fall into the trap of playing along with 'scapegoating' individuals to hold groups together. For example, a group may be rehearsing a play and there is a falling out - should the worker focus on the production or on the relationships? Should, if necessary, the former be sacrificed for the latter? Skilled educators learn to balance these demands. They approach conversation in ways that draw people in, that reduce the isolation of individuals. At a macro level much of their work is directed towards devising events and activities that bring people together or undertaking outreach work to contact those, who for whatever reason, are marginalised.

Talk and conversation

At this point it might be helpful to stop and think some more about the nature of conversation. We are so used to it - so close to it - that we may not appreciate it for what it is.

The first, and obvious, thing to say about talk is that it is a social activity. Apart from talking to yourself, or to animals, we engage in it with others. Much follows from this. To talk with others involves taking into account their feelings, thoughts and needs. In turn, they too must think of you or me. We have to consider, for example, whether our words could upset or offend the others; or whether they will help us in dealing with the matter in hand. Thus, if two or more people are to communicate, then they must:

- Co-operate.

- Think about others' feelings and experiences.

- Give each other room to talk.

In other words, talking - conversation - is a reciprocal process.

Second, conversation involves people agreeing about the topic. There is usually a lot of activity centred on locating an agenda. We have all overheard, and taken part in, talk where each person is intent on his or her topic irrespective of what others are saying. One person might be describing what they have just read in the paper; another talking of his or her feelings concerning a driving test. This is really two monologues - not dialogue.

Third, conversation involves an immediate response. There is not much of a time lag between the action of one person and the response of the other. A number of things flow from this. It means, for example, that what we say may be less thought out. Linked to this is the need for us to be tolerant of what is said to us in the heat of the moment. The immediacy of talk also allows people to ask questions and to explore different angles. However, it can also mean those who fail to respond are viewed with suspicion.

Fourth, although conversation is all around us - it is a very sophisticated activity as Ronald Wardhaugh shows. [12]

You must have a well-developed feeling about what you can (or cannot) say and when you can (or cannot) speak. You must know how to use words to do things and also exactly what words you can use in certain circumstances. And you must be able to supplement

---

[12] Ronald Wardhaugh (1985) *How Conversation Works*, Oxford: Blackwell, page 4.

and reinforce what you choose to say with other appropriate behaviours: your movements, gestures, posture, gaze, and so on. You must also attune yourself to how others employ these same skills.

Reading a list like this brings home why things can often go awry - such as those embarrassing moments when we say 'the wrong thing'. It also enables us to see why so many people feel clumsy, or have difficulties, in this area. Significantly, many of these things are also culturally specific. What is right for one group, may be wrong for another. This means that conversations between people of different cultures require special care.

Fifth, conversation entails certain commitments. For it to work, we have to trust in the others involved. When they say they will do something, for example, then we tend to have to take it at face value. At a minimum we have to be open to the possible truth of their words. We may have doubts - but without a degree of trust and openness to the views of others, conversations (or social life) could not happen. Indeed, effective work must always be based upon participants believing in the truthfulness of the educator. Once that is called into question, and the trust is broken, there is the danger conversation will cease and informal educators will no longer be productive.

Sixth, talk involves us in interpretation - and in filling the gaps. To make sense of what others are saying we often have to make leaps forward. People cannot give us all the information we need right at the start. We put their words in context, make assumptions, and add in material to give shape to what they are saying. For example, a person may start telling us about the problems she is having with her neighbours over noise. To make sense of her anger we have to add in various things, e.g. that her mother is very ill; that there is a history of tension in the street and so on. In other words, conversations often involve people drawing on a large amount of 'background knowledge'. If we do not have it then we have to make great leaps of imagination and hope that all will become clear as the person speaks, or we ask questions.

Finally, we have to acknowledge that conversation is a complex and perplexing activity. It embodies rules and etiquette. It requires participants to possess skills that are improved with practice. Those who lack these can find themselves socially, even physically, isolated. Those who find it difficult to engage in conversation and dialogue inevitably have fewer chances to practice the art so tend to find themselves locked into a vicious circle. Many find conversation difficult to handle. There are those who seem incapable of listening to others; some so self-obsessed they merely deliver a monologue to an unfortunate audience; others who ignore the verbal and visual clues that enable a conversation to flow; and some so competitive they turn each exchange into a battle of wills from which they must emerge victorious. As a result, informal educators must be prepared to teach some of the protocols that underpin the art of conversation. This they may do by example and sensitively devising opportunities for individuals to learn how to listen and participate in dialogue and conversation.

Being with

To fully engage in conversation, we have to be in a certain frame of mind. We have to be with that person, rather than seeking to act upon them. This is of great importance. If we enter into conversation with the desire to act upon the other participants then we are seeing them as objects - things rather than people. It means that we are not able to be fully open to what they are saying. We are not open to interaction. This is something that can happen in our work (and why the authors are not happy with the notion of 'empowerment'). For example, we may see someone putting down another person - and seek to intervene. The temptation is to condemn, to tell the person off, or to make it clear that this is not an acceptable way to behave. This may, indeed, be the best way forward in the situation. However, it may not. We have to take great care of the spirit in which we act - and the way this may be experienced by other people. We need to be ready to listen and ask questions. Nothing is served by arbitrarily closing down conversation. We may feel better or 'cleaner' for having avoided an uncomfortable or objectionable topic, but in doing so we may well have abdicated our responsibilities as educators. Where it is necessary to make our position clear we need to address the act or opinion rather than attack the person.

This leads us to something else that we need to take to heart as informal educators. In the work there is a lot of talk of 'getting inside the other person', of empathizing. At first sight the wish to see things as others do, to 'step into their shoes', seems reasonable. But there are great dangers in this - we do not share their history or their genes.

To imagine we can see the world through other's eyes can be to kid ourselves. It can lead to us acting on what we imagine rather than on what we hear. In this sense, our task is less to understand others as individuals - than to appreciate what they are saying. In other words, we should not be looking at other people, as looking with them at what they are seeking to communicate. There is a similar thought at work when we say things like 'it is not the person I condemn, but the act' - perhaps where someone has committed a serious act of violence against another. Informal educators, like probation or prison officers, must acquire the capacity to work and converse with people whose behaviour may be totally unacceptable to the overwhelming majority or the educator. This is not easy, but such professional distance is essential. If people feel that it is beyond them, then perhaps it is best to find another area of work.

Being open

Conversation for the informal educator is not, then, about trying to win an argument. Rather, conversation is about understanding and learning. This does not mean that we avoid debate and challenge. What it does involve, though, is constantly being open to the possible truth of what others are saying. This makes it a risky business. To be open to what others are saying we have to bring our own beliefs and feelings into play. In other words, we have to enter conversations ready to change our view of things.

However, being open does not mean that we accept everything we hear. We have to make judgements. We are educators, not companion horses. Neither are we simply listeners - as educators we have a responsibility to engage with what is going on. Thus, we will often check:

- We are clear about what is being said.

- The truth of statements.

- The sincerity of the people speaking.

- Whether what is said fits the situation.

All this entails looking for assumptions. It means thinking about the context in which people act and how this has affected them. Further, it involves imagining and exploring alternatives. In short, it means thinking critically; or what two writers called 'crap-detecting'.[13]   They quote Ernest Hemingway. He was once asked if there was one essential ingredient to being a great writer. He replied, 'Yes, there is... a person must have a built-in, shockproof crap detector'. For them the cultivation of 'crap detecting' is the central task of education. Some seem to approach this as a skill, but really it is a frame of mind. We have to be open to what others are saying and ready to subject what is said to certain tests. Keeping a balance between the two is not easy. It depends on our being wise - having the necessary knowledge and developing our ability to make informed judgements. Also, ideas and experiences have to be examined without threatening people's integrity. As part of this we also need to be open to challenge concerning our own experiences, values and ideas.

Going with the flow

We now turn to another quality of conversation - its unpredictability. The way one word follows another, the

---

[13] Neil Postman and Charles Weingartner (1971) *Teaching as a Subversive Activity*, Harmondsworth: Penguin, page 16.

way the subject matter turns this way then that, means that in a very real sense we are often led by conversation rather than leading it. It has a life of its own. Here we can see the extent to which we have to put our trust in conversation. We do not know how it will turn out, but we can have some faith in the process. All conversations have within them some possibility of learning and change. The worry is that their unpredictably can mean that potential is not always realized. The danger then is that we undermine the process.

This can happen in a number of ways. Most obviously, we can fall into the trap of not listening to what people are saying because we label it as trivial. We may dismiss, for example, the endless talk about who has fallen out with whom, or the recounting of incidents that is the staple fare of clubs and groups. We may get frustrated at our inability to engage with people about 'serious issues' such as local housing conditions, their attitude to sex or whatever. Rather than trying to explore why the former topics are important, to go with the flow, we can end up seeking to impose our own agenda. Trying to alter the subject in a conversation is not a problem in itself. But, as educators, we need to take some care about how it may impact on others. It may lead to the other person feeling undervalued or rejected; it may sweep important concerns under the carpet.

Changing conversations

From what has been said it is clear that conversations change. They have beginnings and endings, and can take different forms. There can be a movement from informal chat to serious discussion; from argument to joking. At one point people may simply want information and at another to explore something in depth.

To be successful as informal educators we have to come to terms with the ebbs and flows of conversations. We have to be able to intervene to alter the shape, or form, of what is going on so that people may get the best out of it. In short, it means workers have to be both able to talk and listen; and to manage transitions between various types of, and moments in, conversations. The obvious ones here concern starting and finishing exchanges; and moving between the more informal and formal moments and settings.

At the beginning and end of conversations there can be awkwardness. At the start we have to establish the basis for talk and whether the other person wants to speak to us. Often we will go through a set of routine exchanges - inquiries about friends or family; talking about TV programmes and so on. There are skills of posture and approach that have to be learned if people are going to be comfortable talking to us. Also there must be some shared interests. To work with young men, for example, it is not necessary for us to have a detailed knowledge of football or pretend to be interested in drinking. However, we do need some points in common.

Endings can also be a problem - if they are too abrupt then the charge of rudeness can always be levelled. They have to be negotiated. We should give various signals that the end is approaching. This may be communicated in the way we stand or the direction in which we look. We may apologize - we have 'got to rush'. Explanations are usually required - 'I must go or I'll miss my bus'. However, it may be that the other parties do not recognize our signals. We have to learn to work with those who lack these skills or who choose to make unwarranted demands on our time.

The other major area of transition is between the informal chat and the more formal encounter. The classic examples here are where something very personal or difficult comes up. We may judge that for these to be worked with we need to alter the way, or where, we are talking. For example, it is difficult to properly engage with someone's fears about the death of their father standing in a busy street. Informal educators learn to seize the moment. We may make moves to change the locale of our meeting so that we can 'talk about things properly'. Or we may judge that it is better to talk in such a situation rather than risk losing the opportunity. At other times, we may feel ourselves 'switching' into a different way of talking. What began as a chat with us happily chipping in, may now involve us in taking on a more focused role. The talk becomes more 'serious', we find ourselves speaking less but asking more questions. Some may describe this as switching role, e.g. from conversationalist to counsellor.

Conversations and activities

One of the big problems about conversation is that it has tended to be undervalued by welfare professionals and funders. For example, the education of nurses has focused on the physical care and well-being of patients. Great attention was paid to cleanliness of wards or surgeries, little to the social relationships. Everyday talk is often seen as trivial, as a distraction from 'real' work, or as simply the prelude to more serious issues. The trap here is that in viewing matters this way we overlook how such talk helps build relationships, keeps us sane - and contributes to physical well-being and happiness[14].

The second, major problem is that conversation is set against activity - and, in youth work for example, it is 'activity' that is valued in many settings. At one level contrasting the one with the other is stupid - conversation is an activity. But there is something more at work here - and it is very worrying. More than forty years ago Jalna Hamner[15], when looking at the way young women were excluded from youth provision, noted the same either/or approach. Organized activities such as sports, crafts and discussion groups were seen as 'good'; people sitting talking was 'bad'. She concluded that this sort of attitude works against the interests of young women. In her study (and in those that have followed) young women have consistently valued the chance to sit and talk. Not to recognize this is both sexist and paternalistic. It also shows insecurity on the part of workers

---

[14] For a good discussion of happiness and why we should put it at the centre of what we do see Richard Layard (2005) *Happiness. Lessons from a new science*, London: Penguin / Allen Lane.

[15] Jalna Hamner (1964) *Girls at Leisure*, London: London Union of Youth Clubs.

and their managers. Such conversation is not directed, they do not control it - thus, it is often not seen to be important.

This is not to say that organized activities do not have a role. The chance to take part in, say, sports, to have more formal discussions is a key part of the work. These can provide the stimulus for conversation as well as being enjoyable and developmental in themselves. But we should not let them become the focus for the work, they are simply one aspect. What is more, they are of only limited value if they do not become the focus for conversation. This marks out trainers or coaches from informal educators. For the former winning cups and developing skill will usually be the prime aim. For the latter the opportunity to talk after the event will be the most valuable thing.

Conversation and the group

In the introduction we mentioned Josephine Macalister Brew's book *Informal Education*. She also wrote the excellent *Youth and Youth Groups*.[16] Much of the value to be gained from reading it lies in the way Brew highlights the extent to which informal educators must familiarise themselves with the different ways people conduct themselves within different groups. Brew borrowed many insights from the work of American and British social, club and settlement workers who in the first half of the twentieth century sought to understand how social groups functioned. Social group work, as it was often called, was seen as a primary skill for all informal educators. It was viewed as the way in which social activities, in the words of its foremost pioneers Grace Coyle, could be utilised to 'contribute to the growth of the individual, and the achievement of desirable goals'.[17] Social

---

[16] Josephine Macalister Brew (1957) *Youth and Youth Groups*. London: Faber.

[17] Grace Coyle (1955) 'Definition of the Function of the Group Worker' in H. B. Trecker *Group Work: Foundations and Frontiers*. New York: Whiteside and William Morrow. page 62.

group work has developed into a discrete discipline taught to a range of welfare professionals as group work.

Informal educators predominately operate in places where people gather or meet together. They need groups and, as a consequence, often strive to create them. Having begun to work with a group they may spend a lot of time sustaining it - keeping it healthy and vibrant. The police, community wardens and most members of the public are often dismayed to see a 'gang' of young people gathering outside the chip shop. They may well prefer young people to be out of sight, better at home alone in their bedrooms or watching mindless rubbish on TV than out chatting and laughing. A youth worker undertaking informal education on the streets on the other hand will be generally glad to spy such a gathering as they round the corner. For whilst others may see the young people as a nuisance, a threat to good order and the tranquillity of the neighbourhood, informal educators know that they could have a ready-formed group. Such groups are settings that offer the prospect of engaging in conversation and fostering learning[18].

Being able to connect with that group, however, often demands great expertise. Workers need to know how to relate to the group in a way that makes the likelihood of conversation taking place a possibility. They need to be able to read the dynamics of the group so that they know whether tonight it would be worthwhile stopping to talk or better to walk on by with a cursory nod. They also need to know, for example, which member it might be best to open the conversation with. And when the talk begins, when to be active and when to be inactive; when to be quiet and when to talk; how to encourage and sustain conversation; and how best to include the shy and manage the overly garrulous.

---

[18] A helpful account of the ways in which different members of the community view gatherings of groups of young people and how youth workers can work with them is given by Linda Measor and Peter Squires (2000) *Young People and Community Safety: Inclusion, risk, tolerance and disorder*. Aldershot: Ashgate.

Trusting in conversation

These elements make conversation a powerful focus for educators. Conversation in this sense is not simply a method that we may use; it embodies many of the emotions and virtues we may seek to foster. Through conversation we express concern - by spending time with others we show we are interested in them as well as in what they have to say. We also display trust and respect, we value the other person. More than that, there can be affection. To develop as conversationalists we have to be open to others, to be tolerant and patient.

We can see here in these qualities something that is worth working for, spending a lot of time on. Conversation is an activity to be valued in itself - not just for where it may lead.

Some questions to consider

Reflect on your abilities as a conversationalist. Here are some possible questions:

- Are you someone who is reasonably at ease when meeting new people?

- How do you open up conversations with the people you are working with? What do you say to people you are meeting for the first time?

- Are you open to what others are saying? Do you have a tendency to want to win arguments?

- How happy are you 'going with the flow'?

- Are you able to help people to move from one form of conversation to another, e.g. from social chit chat to more 'serious' talk?

- What are you like on 'endings'?

This is not an exercise that has wrong and right answers. It is more an exercise in self assessment. In a very real sense what we are exploring here is central to our activities as educators. Conversation is both the medium through which we work -

and it involves many of the qualities we seek to foster as educators:

- Concern for others.

- Trust.

- Respect for others - and ourselves.

- Affection.

These themes will be revisited in the next chapter.

Follow up

There are several things you can do to deepen your exploration of conversation and education.

Visit the 'trusting in conversation' support page at www.infed.org/foundations.

Read Mary Wolfe (2001) 'Conversation' in Linda Deer Richardson and Mary Wolfe (eds.) (2001) *The Principles and Practice of Informal Education*, London: RoutledgeFalmer, pages 124-137.

Read 'Engaging in conversation' in Mark K. Smith's (1994) *Local Education*, Buckingham: Open University Press, pages 40-61. This chapter looks at how informal educators approach conversation.

Read Paulo Freire on dialogue in Chapter three of *Pedagogy of the Oppressed*, London: Penguin (1972), pages 60-69. Freire's concept of dialogue is often appealed to – and it is worth reading the original.

Chapter 3

Fostering democracy

Our aims as informal educators change. At one moment we may want to promote talk about home life. At another we may seek to make contact with a group. Yet while aims alter with situations all educators, we argue, must share larger purposes. We must put the cultivation of human flourishing – happiness – at the centre of what we do. As part of this, we argue, educators should pay special attention to fostering democracy and association.

Fellowship

One of the clearest expressions of a concern with happiness in informal education has been a longstanding focus on fellowship. We can see this in the work of many early youth groups, settlements and adult education initiatives. For example, in the early 1900s the Oxford and Bermondsey (Boys') Club founded by Dr. John Stansfeld had *Fratres* (fraternity or brotherhood) as its motto; and the nearby Time and Talents Guild, (who worked with girls and young women) sought 'through fellowship, prayer and service to bring the Spirit of Christ into every part of life'. The process of the London Working Men's College was described as 'friends teaching friends'. [19] Fellowship was seen both as an

---

[19] The significance of fellowship, these examples and R. H. Tawney (see below) is discussed at length in Michele Erina

end of education and a means by which that aim was realized.

This focus on fellowship – commonly understood as a companionship of people on friendly and equal terms – is hardly surprising. Once we recognize that humans are social animals and dependent one on another then the force of William Morris' oft quoted words is clear:

> Forsooth, brethren, fellowship is heaven and lack of fellowship is hell; fellowship is life and lack of fellowship is death; and the deeds that ye do upon the earth, it is for fellowship's sake that ye do them.

For many of the Christian pioneers of informal and adult education fellowship was an extension or expression of God's Kingdom on earth. R. H. Tawney, for example, believed that educators should be looking to transcend the barriers of isolated personalities, 'and become partners in a universe of interests which we share with our fellow-men'. His vision of fellowship, however, was not just confined to close relationships or to membership of a group or association. Tawney wanted to embrace all those in a community. Fellowship, thus, was not just a matter of feelings, 'but as a matter of *right relationships*' which are *institutionally based*'[20]. In other words, fellowship is both a quality of individual relationships, and the organizations and systems of which people are a part. The problem here, as some early workers recognized, was that it was difficult

---

Doyle and Mark K. Smith (forthcoming) *Christian Youth Work. Lessons and legacies.*

[20] The quotation from William Morris is taken from Chapter IV of *A Dream of John Bull*. The Tawney quotation is taken from R. H. Tawney (1966) *The Radical Tradition. Twelve essays on politics, education and literature* (ed. Rita Hinden), Harmondsworth: Penguin Books, pages 87-8. The description of Tawney's vision of fellowship is from Ross Terrill (1973) *R. H. Tawney and His Times. Socialism as fellowship*, Cambridge, Mass.: Harvard University Press, page 199.

to see how capitalism could provide a suitable environment for the formation of 'right relationships'. It tended to generate a 'faith' in acquistiveness and a loss of social cohesion. Not surprisingly, attention was given to the ways in which institutions could become more open and responsive, and trust generated. Fellowship was linked to democracy and the cultivation of association.

Democracy

There are many different ways of running a country, town, community group or club. A leader appointed by others or born to the task like a king might organize things. In the case of a school it might be a head-teacher appointed by governors. Each system has its strengths and in this example you know who is in charge, and decisions may be made efficiently. Many yearn for strong leaders and for others to give direction to their lives. However, there are also great dangers associated with allowing power to be held by a strong leader. It all too easily can lead to abuses of power and to people giving up their responsibilities and surrendering rights - their own and others.

There has been a long and hard struggle to establish more democratic political systems. In part this has been born out of the recognition of the problems and injustices identified above. Democracy encapsulates a belief that everyone, on the basis of their common humanity should 'be treated not merely as objects of legislation, as passive subjects to be ruled, but as autonomous agents who take part in the governance of their own society'[21]. Implicit in this belief is the idea that all are equal citizens. There may remain great inequalities linked to wealth, gender or culture however, a democratic system at least holds out the promise that people can collectively come together to reduce or perhaps even eliminate some or all of those inequalities.

---

[21] Amy Gutmann and Dennis Thompson (2004) *Why Deliberative Democracy?* Princeton, New Jersey: Princeton University Press, page 3.

The relationship between democracy and informal education takes a number of forms. First, democracy opens up greater possibilities for open and honest dialogue. At a national level it is impossible for honest debate to take place in a society where certain views are treated as 'dangerous' and where those who espouse them risk prison or worse. At the level of practice we know that in some settings and institutions where democracy is absent, or severely curtailed, dialogue between those with power and those 'below them' in the hierarchy is generally stilted and sometimes impossible.

Second, and following on from the previous point, democracies provide frameworks and systems that enable dialogue to generate change and reform. The democratic school, like the democratic political party for example, creates forums for debate and most importantly an atmosphere that invites individuals to contribute. Those who fear democracy, by way of contrast, minimise such opportunities and focus attention on the 'leader', the 'head' and the common-sense way of doing things.

Third, democratic systems require an educational infrastructure – formal and informal. Their survival, in part, depends on the existence of an informed and committed electorate. It has to be competent to debate issues, make judgements and to choose the best possible representatives. As a general rule informal educators find it easier to work in open and democratic settings and societies. However, there are many examples where they have and do operate in undemocratic, even oppressive environments. At one level this has involved adapting practice to work in prisons and schools. At another it has led to educators directly challenging oppressive regimes by creating opportunities for dialogue in order to help foster social movements committed to democracy.

Informal educators can have a special role. First, our focus on conversation expresses and fosters values, and ways of being with each other, that are central to democracy. Second, the organizations in which we work for much of the time - clubs, groups, and associations – often have 'democratic' structures. These may not be open or used - but they are there. They provide a chance for learning, and for engaging in politics. In doing this, however, informal educators have to address the relations of power in which they are involved.

Direct democracy

The word 'democracy' has been so used and misused that talk of it ought to set off 'crap detectors' all over the place. That this could happen is not surprising, for to speak of democracy is to approach political power.

Its origins are simple enough. *Demokratia* - meaning 'rule of the people' - was used to describe the way some Greek city-states were governed in the fifth century BC. Citizens took part in regular mass meetings that made decisions about the affairs of the city. Those holding public office only did so for a short period. Sometimes these jobs were taken in turn, at others they were filled by lot or election.

Several things need to happen for such direct participation to work.[22] First, 'ruling and being ruled in turn' depends upon there being equality among the citizens. There has to be an even chance to hold office - and equal voting power. With this also comes liberty. People have to be free to make choices, to live as they may - providing this does not unjustly interfere with others. In other words, democracy requires liberty, and liberty equality.

Second, such 'direct' democracy involves certain commitments. Citizens cannot be passive - for democracy to flourish they must act. They must be ready to take part in meetings; to debate and discuss; to take on public office.

Third, there is the question of scale. The city-states were fairly small - people did not have to travel great distances to meetings; business could take place face-to-face; and the numbers involved manageable. However, numbers were, in part, kept low by excluding the majority of residents. Women and slaves were not citizens. Their exclusion

---

[22] David Held (1996) discusses this in his book *Models of Democracy*, Cambridge: Polity.

reflected their exploitation. The time some men had to be citizens was built on oppression. Others were forced to do their bidding. There are, thus, questions about what we mean by the 'rule of the people'. Who are 'the people' and who is excluded, what areas of life are to be 'ruled', and what happens if we disagree with a rule?

It would be wrong to assume that 'direct' democracy has no place in the modern world; that it is a quaint relic that only survives in backwaters and small organisations. It still thrives in community settings and social movements, some of which have been highly successful. In the United States, especially in New England, many towns and communities run themselves according to this model. Switzerland, which has possibly the highest living standards of anywhere, is organised via a system of cantons and referenda. These, in most respects, retain the key elements pertaining to the concept of direct democracy.

There is a strong tradition within informal education that lays an emphasis upon direct democracy. Within youth work this has found expression in self-determining groups, and in club meetings and 'parliaments'. Within community work it can be found in work with co-operatives and self-help groups.

Representative democracy

Since the seventeenth century in the West, democracy has taken on other meanings. 'Representative democracy' has become a familiar form. Citizens elect politicians and officers to 'represent' their interests and views. As states have grown in scope and scale - so matters have to be managed across great distances. It is one thing for 6000 people to come together in a mass meeting, quite another for 60 million. The abuses and problems with representative forms are well known: politicians and parties take on a life, and interests, of their own; the views of the public can be put on one side for much of the time; and elite's and corruption can flourish.

Of late these problems have been added to in many countries. For example, an emphasis on 'letting the market decide' has been used in some countries to pull back from measures that might protect jobs or wages. At the same time, there has often been an emphasis on developing a strong central state by those in power. This has led to attacks on local democracy and on those who raise awkward questions. This has been joined by other factors including a growing tendency to define many political questions as technical matters. The result is a loss of effective public control over key areas of shared life (such as in health and education). At the same time the gap between those with wealth and those without has widened in many countries. Poverty and homelessness have grown. Similar processes can also be seen at work in the relationships between countries and regions.

To place this fully at the door of governments would be wrong. If the truth were told - many of us have gained in some way. Some of us have got richer - often putting our own needs and wishes (and those of our families and friends) above those of others. Among those who have 'won' there may be a feeling that the losers have got their just deserts; a view of government (and democracy) as a burden; and a tolerance of wide gaps in income.[23] In short, in many countries there has been a stress on private gain as against the common good. One of the ironies in all this is that the rich are not necessarily any happier. Once a certain level of wealth and income is achieved, there appears to be a significant tailing-off of happiness. In market democracies such as Britain and the USA there is now considerable evidence that unhappiness has risen as real income has grown.[24]

These trends provide informal educators with a number of challenges. Fostering democratic processes involves questioning common sense views. Ideas about the naturalness of markets, the right to private gain, and the inevitability of hierarchical structures are woven into daily life. In conversation informal educators have to keep asking,

---

[23] John Kenneth Galbraith (1992) discusses these matters in *The Culture of Contentment*, London: Sinclair-Stevenson.

[24] Robert E. Lane (2000) *The Loss of Happiness in Market Economies*, New Haven: Yale University Press.

for example, what right do 'managers have to manage', experts to decide what is best for others, and employers to control work, training and education? There is a lot of pressure on informal educators to 'behave' themselves, to be 'responsible'. More and more funding for their work is short term and from unaccountable bodies such as lottery boards and health trusts. There is pressure - seen and unseen - to tone down questioning and to quieten those they work with.

Sharing in a common life

Many reading this will be deeply unhappy with this state of affairs. Just how we can change things is another matter - but of one thing we are sure - if change is to be just then we must cultivate democracy.

When we talk of democracy here, we are not only concerned with a way of choosing governments. We look to it as a quality that runs through the whole of life, to the relationships between us. This entails moving beyond a focus on individuals. We are social beings. We are what we are because of our interactions with others. We achieve what we do because we benefit from their work. Thus, if we are all to flourish then we must:

- Recognize that we share many common interests.

- Commit ourselves to consider those interests (and hence the needs of others) when looking to our own.

- Actively engage with, and seek to strengthen, those situations and movements that embody democratic values and draw people together.

In this view, we do not simply add together individuals and get society. People's lives are woven together, we share in a common life. Many ancient Greek thinkers recognized this. Their term for the private individual was *idiotes* (idiot) - such a person was literally a fool as she or he was not interested in public affairs.

Unfortunately, there are major obstacles to us fully sharing in a common life. Deep inequalities in wealth and opportunity work against participation. Democratic virtues have to be fostered in a climate that stresses private gain, the quick buck, and the 'rightness' of those who currently hold power. The very language we use, the words we have, can lead us to think in ways that undermine our shared inheritance. We are taught to respect strong leaders. Uncertainty, doubt and hesitancy are not qualities now held in high regard - however, such virtues are central to democratic debate. For us, debate must influence decision. This presents difficulties for those working in settings where care has to be taken not to stimulate discussion in a way that will lead people unfairly to think they can influence decisions made by others. Examples would include informal educators who work in societies or institutions like prisons and schools where the room for negotiation is limited.

Difference

Sharing in a common life does not mean that we all have to be the same. It involves knowing that we are each dependent on the other. Yet in focusing on what is shared, differences can be overlooked, or put on one side. This can marginalize certain views, and act to oppress various social groups. When talking of nation or community, for example, particular voices and images may dominate. The media may well gloss over or ignore cultural diversity or faces that do not fit the stereotype. Part of our task as informal educators is to question such cosy pictures, to ask why certain voices are not heard.

A further concern is identity. We recognize ourselves as individuals partly through what we share, partly through our differences. Our histories and experiences are unique. The way people label and treat us - for example, because of the colour of our skin, the nature of our religion, where we live or the shape of our bodies - helps to build a sense of ourselves as distinct from others. All sorts of things - good and bad - are linked to this. At the same time, we can come to know that others, perhaps being people of like colour, can have similar experiences. In this way we can come to name ourselves - to say we are like this or that. We can also say what we are not and what it may be possible to change. Such concerns have been central to the development of anti-oppressive practice within informal education.

Naming ourselves is one matter, learning to live and engage with diversity is another. As informal educators know, if people do not have a grip on who or what they are, or if there is change, then they can feel lost. When familiar landmarks are gone, we may not know where to place ourselves. There are also pressures to conform with dominant beliefs and ways of life. To stand outside these draws attention, it can disrupt daily routines. What is more, if we do not take up certain ways of behaving, then we can be excluded from groups, from access to work and so on. Here we have another aspect of anti-oppressive work. Educators need to work so that people can be more comfortable with change and diversity; and to question exclusion. Is exclusion, for example, built on prejudice, or the desire to keep power or resources in particular hands? Equally, we must ask ourselves why we support or oppose separate provision for certain groups. In whose interest does it work? Does it encourage exclusion or erode it?

We should not play down the pressures to conform or the difficulties of dealing with difference. However, one thing we can work out fairly easily is that if people are to enjoy a humane and common life then they must engage with each other - and allow each other to be different. And it is here that we can see the special contribution of informal educators. Their task involves encouraging dialogue. This can be painful and awkward. Differences cannot always be reconciled. Respect for children's rights, for example, cannot be easily squared with the religious beliefs of some parents. Informal educators are often working in dangerous areas in this respect. They must also take special care as they do not always have to bear the consequences of the changes they initiate.

Conversation

As we saw in Chapter 2, conversation allows us to come to some understanding about the feelings and beliefs of others. We can, through talk, begin to map out those matters upon which we agree and differ. What is more, to engage in conversation is to express certain values and emotions.

Conversation is, at heart, a social relationship. It entails people working together. There has to be reciprocity and a chance for everyone to participate. Openness to the possible truth of what the other is saying is also required. This has an 'emotional' side. Conversation involves:

- **Concern.** To be with people, engaging them in conversation involves commitment to each other. We feel something for the other person as well as the topic.

- **Trust.** We have to take what others are saying in good faith. This is not the same as being gullible. While we may take things on trust, we will be looking to check whether our trust is being abused.

- **Respect.** While there may be large differences between partners in conversation, the process can only go on if there is mutual regard.

- **Appreciation.** Linked to respect, this involves valuing the unique qualities that others bring.

- **Affection.** Conversation involves a feeling with, and for, those taking part.

- **Hope.** We engage in conversation in the belief that it holds possibility. Often it is not clear what we will gain or learn, but faith in the process carries us forward. [25]

Such feelings are central to conversation - and they also have to be present if democracy is to flourish. Educators, by emphasizing conversation, help to build relationships in which people are ready to listen to, and work with each other. As the focus lies upon coming to some greater understanding rather than winning the argument there is greater hope of handling difference - of working so that

---

[25] Nicholas C. Burbules (1993) *Dialogue in Teaching*, New York: Teachers College Press.

people with contrasting cultures and orientations can come to share in a common life.

Genuine conversation is difficult in unequal relationships. For example, it may be difficult to have a truly open exchange of views between a prison officer and a prisoner; a schoolteacher and a pupil; a doctor and a nurse. In these sorts of settings it can take great skill, commitment and courage on the part of both to say what they believe and to expose weakness or doubt. Informal educators have to be sensitive. They have to appreciate the way they may be seen and experienced. They must be prepared to negotiate around relationships of power. These will never go away - but they can be partially changed to the benefit of the prisoner, the pupil and the nurse.

Association

The setting for much of our work as informal educators is a special kind of group. For example, we may be working in church or community groups, or in enthusiast or interest groups. The latter may be in schools and colleges or free standing. They could be focused around sports, the arts, or enthusiasms such as gardening or computing. There are several things about such groups that make them good sites for education - and can help to build democratic communities.

First, these groups usually have an associational structure. That is to say, institutions such as churches, tenants groups, village halls and enthusiast groups have elected officers and committees. They also have other ways of giving space so members can have a say. Such local groups are also often part of a national organization or movement. As such they allow people to come together to influence larger political processes. Local groups are the means through which most of us engage with the traditional political arena. By encouraging people to become involved in the running of such groups, we help them to enter organized politics; to engage in public life.

Second, such groups usually involve a commitment to others. They carry within them some valuing of cooperation, and some readiness to help other members. When we join a fishing club or church, for example, we are admitting that our own pleasure or well-being depends on our acting with others. For this to happen, as we saw above, there has to be some commitment. Further, such readiness to work with, and help others usually goes beyond the initial or immediate focus of the group. If someone is ill or is going through a 'difficult time' then there may be some expectation among members that they should help.

Third, many groups are mutual aid organizations. They involve people joining together to produce goods and services for their own enjoyment and use. Relationships are informed by ideas of 'give and take'. Groups may range from swimming clubs to bee-keeping societies and stamp collecting circles; from farming or allotment associations to basketball teams. While an enthusiasm or interest may provide a focus for activity, such groups are far from being wholly concerned with 'doing things'. Much of the reason for their success is that they also fulfil social needs.[26]

Last, and linked to the above, such groups help provide a sense of belonging and identity as well as a setting to meet and make friends with people. In saying who or what we are we often make reference to the groups to which we belong. Even the routine activities of such groups, e.g. around catering, meetings and finance, provide us with ways of shaping our world.

In Britain alone there are said to be well over a million voluntary groups - possibly many more - involving between 12 and 25 million people in their running. The life of these associations provide many opportunities for learning. Aside from the learning linked to their overt purpose - to pursue specialist interests, provide support, advocate and represent - they also provide opportunities for people to develop their organizing skills, confidence and their readiness to take on

---

[26] These matters are discussed by Jeff Bishop and Paul Hoggett (1986) *Organizing Around Enthusiasms. Mutual aid in leisure*, London: Comedia.

responsibility.[27] What is more, each is a small democracy. Each involves direct participation and the chance for people to share in making decisions about the things that affect their common life. They offer a means to extend and give life to democracy, to bring decision-making closer to people.

Unfortunately there is growing evidence that such associational activity in on the decline in market democracies. One large influential study in the USA, for example, has revealed a significant decline in the active membership of clubs and groups. While a number of things appear to have contributed to this, the researchers single out the development of suburban sprawl and rise of home-based entertainment (especially television).[28] The same study has shown that there are considerable benefits in terms of health, educational achievement and economic activity linked to those communities where there is a strong tradition of associational activity. (The researchers talk about this in terms of 'social capital' by which they mean the connections among individuals, social networks and the norms of reciprocity and trustworthiness that arise from them). It is for this reason that some policymakers have started looking again to the contribution that local groups can make and the role that informal educators such as youth workers and community educators might have.

Informal educators, association and democracy

There has been a long history of informal educators working in co-operatives and community associations, and in youth and church organizations. The social, educational and political potential has long been recognized. Yet, there have also been strong pressures for play workers, youth workers, community educators and others, to slip into becoming

---

[27] See K. T. Elsdon with John Reynolds and Susan Stewart (1995) *Voluntary Organizations. Citizenship, learning and change*, Leicester: NIACE, pages 39 and 67.

[28] Robert D. Putnam (2000) *Bowling Alone. The collapse and revival of American community*, New York: Simon and Schuster.

providers of opportunities - activities, classes, groups; or to focus on the needs of individuals. There are demands from managers to meet targets for the numbers of people worked with; and to address government requirements to work with those 'not in employment, education or training' ('NEETs').

Struggling with the ups and downs of associational life can be time consuming and wearing. It is easy to see it as chore rather than an opportunity. As Josephine Macalister Brew once said: 'A club is neither a series of individuals... nor is a club a club leader. A club is a community engaged in the task of educating itself'.[29] Our task as educators is to work alongside people so that they may learn and organize things for themselves. This is a major challenge for many of us. Coming to terms with informal education involves containing the impulse to always be the provider. There will be times when we do put on special activities and groups. For much of the time, though, our central concern should be to work with others so that they may organize and take responsibility.

In this chapter we have tried to show something of what informal educators can do to foster democracy and association. However, before we leave this subject, we want to make one further point. These matters are not marginal to our task as educators - they are central. The cultivation of the knowledge, skills and virtues necessary for participation in public life - is arguably more important morally than any other purpose of public education in a democracy.[30] Yes, people do need to learn various skills related to work and to home life. Yes, people do need to develop their intellects so that they may add to the sum of human knowledge. But more important than these is learning to engage with each

---

[29] Josephine Macalister Brew (1943) *In the Service of Youth*, London: Faber, page 67.

[30] Amy Gutmann (1987) *Democratic Education*, Princeton: Princeton University Press, page 287. Nel Noddings argues that this is not enough – we also need to look to caring and private life. See her (2002) *Starting at Home. Caring and social policy*, Berkeley: University of California Press.

other in ways that display mutual respect, a concern for others needs, and a belief in community. For without this, such democracy as we have will be subverted, and oppression will flourish. When that happens education serves the interests of the few. Informal educators cannot, therefore, be neutral. Our behaviour and attitudes must convey deep respect for democratic values. Within our practice we must seek to build, not destroy, democracy and association.

Some questions to consider

1. Here we have placed a special emphasis on democracy - or as Dewey put it: working so that people may share in a common life. How would you describe the aims of your work?

2. Do you work in ways that encourage people to join in and to take the responsibility for organizing things? Think about this with regard to your work over the last few weeks.

3. Gaining a sense of identity involves looking at what we share with others, and how we are different. Consider the recent conversations you have had with a couple of individuals. Have you attended to both elements? Have you linked this questions of identity?

4. To what extent are the groups you work with 'communities in the task of educating themselves?'

5. What are educators to do in societies that discourage democratic ways of living?

6. What would be the result if you applied a 'democratic audit' to the pieces of work you are involved in. For example, do they:

   • enable all to share in a common life?

   • encourage people to think critically?

   • foster the values and attitudes of a free society?

- sustain and extend opportunities for political participation?

- contribute towards greater equality?

Follow up

There are several things you can do to deepen your exploration of democracy and informal education.

Visit the 'fostering democracy' support page at www.infed.org/foundations for further discussion, examples, activities and links.

Read John Dewey's 'The democratic conception in education' [Chapter 7 of his (1916) book *Democracy and Education*, New York: The Free Press, pages 81-99]. This has been a very influential statement and can be found on the support page.

Read the opening chapters of Robert D. Putnam (2000) *Bowling Alone. The collapse and revival of American community*, New York: Simon and Schuster. There is a profile of Putman on the support page, plus lots of material on social capital, learning and association.

Read chapters 4 and 5 of Amy Gutmann and Dennis Thompson (2004) *Why Deliberative Democracy?* Princeton, New Jersey: Princeton University Press. The first of these explains what deliberative democracy is. The second looks at the way in which it operates in order to organise the distribution of scarce health resources.

Chapter 4

Exploring reflection and learning

So far we have seen that informal educators work in a variety of settings; that they organize their work around conversation; and that they have a special contribution to make in fostering democracy and association. In this chapter we want to return to the question of learning - and how we go about deepening people's thinking.

Emancipating and enlarging experience

John Dewey once wrote that the 'business of education might be defined as an emancipation and enlargement of experience'.[31] As educators most of us can identify with these words. For example, we may describe parts of our work in terms of 'learning by doing' and of widening opportunities, or giving people new experiences. Yet, Dewey meant something more than this.

When we talk of 'enlarging' the meaning is fairly clear. We usually mean that we want to make something bigger - to extend its limits. With regard to experience this is not just a matter of widening, of encouraging people to do different things, it also involves deepening. By this we mean that as

---

[31] John Dewey (1933) *How We Think,* New York: D. C. Heath, page 340.

educators our task is to work with people so that they may have a greater understanding or appreciation of their experiences. For example, the way in which we may work with a group to plan a foreign visit would be significantly different from the way we would plan a holiday. The prime purpose of the first is learning, the second relaxation.

Again, the meaning of 'emancipation' need not trouble us - it is a process of setting free. But what does it mean to set free experience? Here we touch on the profound. It is easy to fall into seeing experiences as things. After all, we often talk of 'having an experience', of things 'happening to us'. In this we get a picture of being on the receiving end of some event. Yet this is only half the story. Experiences are not only 'had', they are also 'known'. By this we mean that they are thought about at some level, although we may not be conscious of this. We interpret what is going on and this allows us to be 'set free' - we need not be dictated to by, or victims of, experience. We can become not just 'experiencers' but also experimenters: creators as well as consumers.

Experience entails thought. It includes reflection. To emancipate and enlarge experience, we must attend to both having and knowing.

The nature of reflection

When we use the word 'reflection' we usually want to describe a process of thought that is active and careful. It is an activity in which people 'recapture experience', mull it over and evaluate it. David Boud and his associates suggest that it involves three aspects:

- *Returning to experience* - that is to say recalling or detailing salient events.

- *Attending to (or connecting with) feelings* - this has two aspects: using helpful feelings and removing or containing obstructive ones.

- *Evaluating experience* - this involves re-examining experience in the light of one's aims and knowledge. It also entails integrating this new knowledge into one's conceptual framework.[32]

As informal educators, part of our task is to foster environments in which people can look to their experiences. To do this we also need to look to our own.

Returning to experience

When we talked earlier of remembering - we tried to show how the process of 'looking back' is not quite like opening a filing cabinet. In files we have physical objects that can be retrieved in the same form as we put them in the drawer (provided no one else has been using them!) With memory we have something more tenuous. We cannot dig into our memory and extract thoughts in the same way as we first had them. Two things are specially worth looking at here. First, looking back entails building an impression of what occurred. It is an active process. We have to 'go back over' events - and what we look for depends strongly on the situation that is currently occupying us. For example, we may be trying to deal with a young man who is being very aggressive. To do this we may draw on things that have happened in the past. Because our immediate concern is to deal with his aggression we look back specifically for things that may help us with this task. We do not remember all the experiences we have had with him or every aspect of similar situations. We try to focus on what might be of direct use. Memory is a process of thinking, of selection and building.

Second, what we remember, the sense we make of things, is generally shaped by how we are feeling at the time. When we are happy we tend to look to the good times, when sad the bad. We are, what the social psychologists call, 'state dependent'. For this reason alone we need to attend to our feelings - past and present.

---

[32] David Boud, Rosemary Keogh and David Walker (1985) *Reflection: Turning experience into learning*, London: Kogan Page, pages 26-31.

In conversation informal educators may ask questions that help people to look back at what happened. We may simply encourage them to tell the story. We are also likely to ask questions about, or point to, the things that may be significant in their story.   We may ask 'what were you thinking when you did that?' or 'what was it about the situation that made you so angry?' We can make statements: 'From what you say it seems you found that what he did was very wrong'. Often where strong feelings are involved, our main task at this point is to help people entertain these emotions. That is to say to work with them so that they can name and own these feelings. This can be a profoundly draining and time consuming process. We have to judge what is involved and take care to predict the potential demands that may be made upon us. This is central to the job.

Attending to feelings

As educators we may talk about 'sensing situations' or 'having a feeling that something would happen'. We may describe this as intuition or as working from 'gut feelings'. These are an important aspect of our work. We have to respond to situations quickly, to think on our feet. In that split second it is not possible to carefully review matters, to look to possible courses of action, and to make decision about how to act.

A question to ask here is what is the nature of the 'sensing' in these situations? We suspect that much that we put down to intuition or 'gut feelings' is, rather, the product of those thinking processes of which we are barely conscious. Through 'habit' or what Freud called a 'preconscious' thought we may recognize in this situation some pattern that we have seen in the past. In so doing, we are then able to begin to make sense of what is happening.

Feelings are significant for other reasons - they are, after all, part of what it is to be human. They help to drive us. Monitoring them can bring great insight. For example, attending to the way someone is 'making us feel' can give us some sense of what might be happening for them in other situations. This is why supervision, recording and talking to colleagues is so important. Each of these encourages us to reflect on our own experiences, to look to our own feelings, thoughts and actions. Without engaging with these it can be very difficult to work with others. Conversations with our peers around these matters must not be seen as time-wasting. Such activities are an essential part of our work. Within them we rehearse ideas and evaluate practice.

Here we have been focusing on our processes as informal educators. But attending to feelings is similarly important when working with others to further understanding. In helping people to make sense of why they acted in this way or that we may ask about their feelings then and now. We can also encourage such reflection by making sure that we are using words to draw attention to feelings. We may say things like, 'if I had been in the same situation I think I would have been very angry' or 'I guess you felt pretty crappy at that moment'.

We have to take care to find words that may help the person to articulate their feelings. In this there is a danger that we may not speak for fear of saying the wrong thing. In these circumstances it is perhaps helpful to remember that in conversation you do not always have to get the right word - simply the one that furthers exploration. The person might not have felt 'crappy' at that moment - but, if the spirit of conversation is there, she or he can ask why we thought that; or can correct what we have said. We have to learn to make professional judgements about appropriate and inappropriate interventions. Informal educators must read settings and behaviours. They need to learn when humour is required and when it is misplaced; when conversation is desirable and when silence is needed.

Making connections and judgements

Returning to experience and attending to feelings involves interpretation. Now we want to look at making connections and judgements. In conversation we look to what can be learned.

When examining intuition, we suggested that in looking at something that is happening now, we can draw on ideas, images and memories of events. These are not exactly the same as what is occurring now or what we may be looking at, but they provide us with a starting point, a way of making sense. We can then play with them, adapt and develop them to fit the new. We make connections. Again the important thing to point out here is that making connections is a matter of imagination. Memories have to be built and searched, we have to see if this situation can be altered to fit that. We have to encourage people to open their minds to various possibilities and to make links. Then there is the question of judgement. Interpretation inevitably involves coming to some decisions as to whether something fits, whether it is valid. Here we can look to the sort of questions we suggested with regard to crap detecting.

Reflection-in-action and reflection-on-action

A further, helpful distinction made by Donald Schön is between reflection-in-action and reflection-on-action. The former can be thought of as 'thinking on our feet'. In other words, we are able to think about the situation as it is happening, and to fashion our response. Another way of putting it is as reflecting in time to act. Reflection-on-action is something that happens after the event. As workers, for example, we write journals and keep records, talk to others and think about the way we have dealt with situations. We are then able to feed this into the way we work with similar situations and experiences in the future. Reflection-in-action happens relatively quickly. As a result our responses are not likely to be as considered as when we reflect-on-action. Some might argue that this means we shouldn't call it 'reflection'. However, 'thinking on our feet' has the great merit of our being able act and to then gauge the other person's reactions and to further adjust our behaviour. Over the time we are in the situation or engaging in a conversation it is thus possible to return to experience, attend to feelings and make connections and judgements. We can also pick up on them afterwards.

All this involves a circle of inquiry:

It is initiated by the perception of something troubling or promising and it is determined by the production of changes one finds on the whole satisfactory or by the discovery of new features which give the situation new meaning and change the nature of the questions to be explored.[33]

This circle of inquiry is also something that we look to cultivate with those with whom we work and in ourselves as workers. Part of our focus as educators is to enhance people's ability to appreciate and judge their experiences and learning.[34]

Learning from experience

A well-known way of describing this process is as experiential learning (*See Figure 4.1*). The process begins with a person carrying out an action and then seeing the effect of the action on and in the situation. Following this, a second step is to understand these effects in the situation. This is so that if the same action were taken in similar circumstances it would be possible to anticipate what would follow from the action. In the third step these observations and reflections are then brought together into a 'theory' from which new implications for action can be worked out. The last step is then to use the 'theory' as a guide to acting in a new situation.

We can see that the stages in this model link to the various elements we have already discussed. Concrete experience is used to validate and test abstract concepts or 'theories'. This is made possible by feedback from the situation. Here these steps are shown as a circular movement. In reality, these things may be happening all at once. Furthermore, if learning has taken place then, as Kurt Lewin put it, such a process could be seen as a spiral of

---

[33] Donald A. Schön (1983) *The Reflective Practitioner. How professionals think in action*, London: Temple Smith, page 151.

[34] See Elliot W. Eisner (1998) *The Enlightened Eye. Qualitative inquiry and the enhancement of educational practice*, Upper Saddle River, NJ: Merrill, page 80.

steps, 'each of which is composed of a circle of planning, action, and fact-finding about the result of the action.'[35]

Figure 4.1: Experiential learning (after Lewin and Kolb) [36]

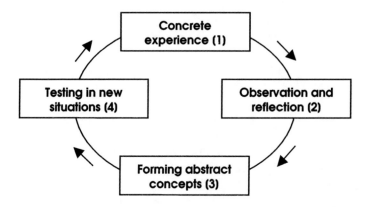

If we apply this to, say, some work we may be doing with a group around their relationships with their carer(s) or parent(s) - we can see how it fits together. We may begin by asking people to return to situations and attend to their feelings [2]. We can then encourage them to make links with other relationships and situations; or to things that have happened previously. From there we may be able to help them to make judgements and begin to build theories about why they act in this way or that [3]. We can then encourage them to think about what they may do differently when, say, faced with their carer(s) or parent(s) demanding that they act in this way or that. They then take that into a future

---

[35] Kurt Lewin (1948) *Resolving Social Conflicts*, New York: Harper and Row, page 206.

[36] This diagram is a version of one included in David Kolb (1984) *Experiential Learning*, Englewood Cliffs: Prentice Hall. The circle he is describing here was first put forward by Kurt Lewin with regard to action research and groupwork.

situation [4] - which in turn stimulates further reflection and thought.

Some problems

This is a helpful way of looking at the situations we face as educators. However, it has problems - four of which we want to mention.

First, this approach uses the idea of steps or stages in thinking. Stage four follows three which follows two and so on. In fact, things may not be so clear cut. They overlap and interconnect; the order changes; and we may pay more attention to some aspects than to others. As John Dewey argued, in thinking there is flux and a constant flood of impressions. Right from the start our thoughts may jump to possible solutions. No set rules can be laid down on such matters. We, thus, should not rely too heavily on the mechanical sequence. We should not worry too much if, at times, conversation hops back and forth, or if we seem to spend a lot of time on one aspect. We can use ideas such as this to review what is going on - but we have to guard against thinking that thought has to follow some set pattern. As Josephine Macalister Brew once stressed, informal educators must be prepared to plunge in at 'the point which has attracted their attention' and thereafter be willing to work 'either backwards or forwards according to how' those with whom we are working respond.[37] Having to revisit a topic should not be interpreted by informal educators as an indication of failure - 'if only I had explained it better they would not be raising it again'. Rather it must be often more correctly understood as those we engaged with wishing to continue the dialogue. They might want to clarify their thinking or to contest the validity of our previous position. Instead of being dismayed we should be delighted that the seed sown is germinating.

---

[37] Josephine Macalister Brew (1946) *Informal Education: Adventures and Reflections*. London: Faber.

Second, there is always a danger in this sort of model, and in education generally, of trying to get to the 'end'. In this case the 'end' could be the generation of new knowledge (at least this is how Kolb viewed it). Trying to push people too fast into this area is a common mistake. We often need time to entertain feelings and ideas. Jumping over, or ignoring this dimension can mean that little is actually achieved. Further, one of the great features of a circular or spiral model is that there is no ending - as we discover something this becomes a spur to further experimentation. Alternatively, people may experience no immediate learning or recognition, and it is only later, sometimes much later, that the value is recognized.

Third, some educators fall into the trap of thinking that for any one person or group all they need to do is to provide an opportunity for experience which is then followed by time for reflection and theory making. The other side of the coin in this approval is a put-down of 'book-learning' or the worth of formal educational experiences, lectures and talks. There has been a tendency in some areas of informal education to undervalue such forms. This has contributed to a lack of attention to recording practice and theory making. As we will see later, the literature on informal education is thin. However, this is no excuse for ignoring it and failing to build upon it.

We should not, further, fall into the trap of thinking that informal education is solely about learning from experience. It also entails giving information. We have to respect the wishes of those we work with. This can mean that on occasions individuals or groups may only need or want knowledge or advice - not exploration. For example, an older person may simply want to know about changes in pensions - and all we need to do is to respond with that information. We have no right to oblige them to engage in conversation as the 'payment' for access to such knowledge.

Fourth, to build theories about an experience we need to draw on a repertoire of ideas and images. We can make things happen much more quickly for us if we have ideas to draw upon and ways of getting at them. 'Book-learning' and teaching can give us access to a range of theories and ways of making sense. In other words, we need to recognize that a 'starting point' for a lot of our efforts may not be concrete experience, but rather the giving of information. This then leads to reflection, theory-making, and then application to a specific problem. This brings us back to our original point - gaining information, returning to experience, attending to feelings, building theory and acting in situations are all aspects of an ever-changing process. We should not assume that a particular sequence is the one we should always follow or will encounter. Nor should we assume that we must always construct our own theories. The thinking and ideas of those who went before can serve us well in many situations. The task of informal educators is not to passively allow people 'learn from their mistakes'. That can be costly. It is, where appropriate, to act as a clearing-house, linking people to ideas, theories and knowledge which will serve them well. It is to function as a bridge between the experiences of those who went before and the present.

Some implications

These problems should not detract from the usefulness of the model. In our conversations we can help people to make sense of things by looking with them at experiences. We can explore what happened; we can examine feelings; and we can work on making connections; forming judgements and fitting new understandings in with what they already know. More than that, we can work with people so that they can work out possible moves. In this way we may help them to engage with new situations; and to interact with others.

As we have seen, informal educators devote the bulk of their energies to encouraging learning by methods not typically seen in schools and colleges. Although at times they may turn to the instructional methods lecturers and schoolteachers mainly employ this is not the norm. Put simply informal educators make use of different techniques. This difference in approach has led many to assume that informal educators are not teachers. We believe this is mistaken. Teachers are to be found wherever people gather. To teach, to help others learn and be willing to pass on knowledge and experience to others is a component of being human. Of course if one picks up a book with 'Teacher' in the title it will almost inevitably be about working within a school or college. It is one of the tragedies of our time that teaching is now mostly talked about as a paid activity ensnared within classrooms. This needs challenging, not least by us as informal educators.

As informal educators we are seeking to 'lead people out' towards understanding and discernment. As such we create and exploit opportunities for others, and ourselves, to learn. In other words, we intervene to teach. We may not call registers, use whiteboards or 'deliver' a curriculum, but we teach - not in classrooms but in the world. This we do primarily through conversation and example. Our concern is to build 'bridges between concrete, everyday ideas and more abstract, academic concepts',[38] to foster critical thinking. As informal educators we are seeking to identify and problematize the experiences of others; to teach by example and to reflect back those experiences for scrutiny through conversation. Informal educators are not the sort of teachers Michael Oakeshott dubbed 'dancing masters'. Rather he describes teaching as follows:

> To teach is to bring it about that, somehow, something of worth intended by a teacher is learned, understood and remembered by a learner. Thus, teaching is a variegated activity which may include hinting, suggesting, urging, coaxing, encouraging, guiding, pointing out, conversing, instructing, informing, narrating, lecturing, demonstrating, exercising, testing, examining, criticising, correcting, tutoring, drilling and so on - everything, indeed, which does not belie the engagement to impart an understanding. And learning may be looking, listening, overhearing, reading, receiving suggestions, submitting to guidance, committing to memory, asking questions,

---

[38] C. Meyers (1986) *Teaching Students to Think Critically: A guide for faculty in all disciplines.* San Francisco: Jossey-Bass.

> discussing, experimenting, practising, taking notes, recording, re-expressing, and so on - anything which does not belie the engagement to think and to understand.[39]

To observe an expert informal educator at work is to witness someone employing all the artistry outlined above - but without the legal sanctions a schoolteacher has to enforce attendance or attention. Once we discard the prejudice that the only real teachers are schoolteachers and focus instead upon the essence of 'teaching' it becomes difficult to see the informal educator as anything but a teacher. Albeit one who is fortunate to be working largely 'beyond the classroom'.

As informal educators we should not, thus, shy away from giving information where the situation demands it. Many, such as health promoters, street workers and advice workers have developed substantial expertise in their areas. Those they work with can rightly value their knowledge. It also allows them to engage in conversations and ask questions that would be unacceptable or intrusive if initiated by others. We need to recognize the significance of expertise - informal education is not pure process. For example, health visitors may be able to engage in conversation about highly personal matters because they are seen as possessing expert knowledge. They also bring with them a clear expectation of confidentiality.

We should not ignore the need for more 'traditional' and formal forms such as encouraging reading or giving talks. The provision of information is a necessary part of our task. We need, also, to take care to avoid labelling ourselves as 'experiential educators' - this wrongly narrows what we do to a particular method. Rather, our concern with experience involves its emancipation and enlargement.

---

[39] Michael Oakeshott ((1972) 'Education: the engagement and its frustration' in R. F. Dearden, P. H. Hirst and R. S. Peters (eds.) *Education and the Development of Reason*. London: Routledge and Kegan Paul pages 25-6.

Some questions to consider

1. Reflection involves returning to experience; attending to feelings; and evaluating experience. Consider some recent conversations you have had in your work. Have all three elements been present? Have you worked so that people can attend to each?

2. Consider the picture of experiential learning in *Figure 4.1*. Compare it with a recent piece of work with a group or an individual. How well does it fit what occurred? What seems different?

3. Often our work is such that we are only able to go so far with people. We are interrupted; we only have a short time with people - and so on. How do you handle this as an educator? What do you do with your feelings?

4. Do you spend enough time reflecting on your own work?

Follow up

There are several things you can do to deepen your exploration of reflection and learning.

Visit the 'reflection and learning' support page at www.infed.org/foundations for further discussion, examples, activities and links.

Read David Boud, Rosemary Keogh and David Walker's chapter 'Promoting reflection in learning' in their (1985) book *Reflection: Turning experience into learning*, London: Kogan Page. It is a clear introduction to the process.

Read John Dewey's classic discussion of reflective thinking – Chapter five of (1933) *How We Think*, Boston: D. C. Heath. An e-text of this chapter can be found through the support page.

Chapter 5

Working with process

Some reading these words will have been on one of the growing number of training programmes that approach our work much like a vehicle road-worthiness test. They are based on the idea that all we have to do to be good play, youth, community or community education workers is to gain and use certain skills and knowledge. We think informal educators are more than mechanics working to some plan. Rather we are creative artists - able to improvise and devise new ways of looking at things. Like artists we help, even demand, others look at the world in fresh and challenging ways.

This might sound odd but all we would ask is you think about those educators whom you think are good. What stands out about them? The sorts of qualities that we hear commonly mentioned are 'being able to relate to people'; 'to think on their feet'; 'able to make things happen', and 'to share their thinking and feelings with others'. To do this we have to know certain things, and to be able to draw on a range of techniques, but there is more to it than that.

Working with

People are not machines or objects that can be worked on like motor cars. They have to be worked with. Our relationships are human and as such involve all sorts of emotions and values. We engage with situations that are each different in some way, and often messy and unpredictable. The thing that makes us special as educators is the way in which we are able to draw on our skills and knowledge, to inform these by a commitment to work for what is good, to improvise, and be ourselves. It is this quality that we call artistry.

To think about these matters we begin with a simple diagram that shows education as a sort of production line (*Figure 5.1*). If we think about something like health promotion we can see how this might work. The input might be people who have little or no knowledge about what makes for a healthy diet. Through engaging in a process with others (including us as educators) they become more aware of diet and different types of food. The outcome, hopefully, would be people who are more aware of what healthy eating comprises.

Figure 5.1: Input - process - outcome

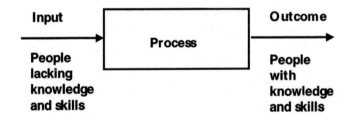

Looking at the diagram above can help us focus on two very different approaches to educating. One is concerned with outcomes (a product approach) and the other with interaction (a process approach). As we will see, the process approach can either be made formal via a curriculum or driven by dialogue. However, let's begin by looking at product approaches.

Product approaches

These approaches are derived from ways of thinking that are common in industry and commerce. We start out by trying to define closely what sort of output or product we want to make. If we were manufacturing a car, for example, we would do some market research (identify needs); make plans (of the car, its production and marketing); implement the plans; and then check whether what we have produced matches our original objectives. It seems so sensible and is a very common way of going about things. We can see the sense in it if we are trying to make something concrete like a car. We need a plan that people can have access to, so that they can go off and make their particular part so it will fit with other parts.

We can find this product approach in the way that many people talk about curriculum in schooling. A curriculum is just one way of organizing the work of educators. It is a proposal for action - something we build before the educational encounter. *Figure 5.2* shows a fairly common approach to planning a product curriculum.

Figure 5.2: Planning the product curriculum

Step 1:   Diagnosis of need

Step 2:   Formulation of objectives

Step 3:   Selection of content

Step 4:   Organization of content

Step 5:   Selection of learning experiences

Step 6:   Organization of learning experiences

Step 7:   Determination of what to evaluate and of the ways and means of doing it.

Taken from Hilda Taba (1962) *Curriculum Development: Theory and practice*, New York: Harcourt Brace, page 12.

Such an approach has problems. First, if we define closely what learners will learn before the encounter, then we limit the opportunity for dialogue. Consider, for example, the pressure on teachers in many countries to complete the national curriculum. In order to prepare their 'pupils' for the tests that measure whether or not they have completed the various stages, teachers have to severely limit the chance of free-flowing discussion. Opportunities for group working and creative learning have to be sacrificed. The curriculum determines not just what is learnt, but also to a large extent how the learning takes place.

Second, in conversation the focus can change and different things become important. Participants can express their needs. This is difficult, and sometimes impossible, in a product approach. For example an informal educator working in a residential home for older people might start out assuming that people would welcome the chance to reminisce and to connect with their past. The residents, however, may have very different ideas as to their needs or interests. It is often tricky to rectify quickly a misdiagnosis of need when locked into a concern with product.

Third, product approaches can quickly slip into educators defining outcomes for learners and, thus, be anti-democratic. If we look at schooling again we can see where this leads. As informal educators often discover, attempts to democratize institutions by establishing school councils and consultative bodies rarely succeed. The key purpose of the institution and those things that occupy most of the young people's time, for example what is taught, are excluded from democratic control. These bodies are reduced to picking over the trivia of school life.

We can see from this that product-based approaches tend to involve working on, not with, people. The focus is on changing individuals in ways set out by others. It entails teaching them the skills and attributes which employers, politicians and opinion leaders hold to be desirable. Sadly, this orientation has spread beyond settings such as schools and colleges. Many of the activities that play, youth and community education workers are responsible for are now product-oriented. Programmes such as the Youth Achievement Awards, and targeted efforts to tackle crime, truancy, drug usage, under-achievement, unemployment and social exclusion are examples here. They may well employ some of the techniques of informal education. They can even appear to be informal education. However, they are not. They are not driven by dialogue. Anti-conversational and anti-democratic tendencies mean that product approaches are incompatible with informal education.

A process approach to curriculum

Many readers will have come across talk of a process curriculum. As we have already seen, a curriculum is something that is devised ahead of an educational encounter. It is a proposal for action. A process approach to curriculum does not specify outcomes in advance. It looks to the qualities of interaction that occur in an educational situation. Rather than having objectives about what people should learn, as in a product curriculum, it has a general aim or intention. A traditional curriculum may set out in some detail the knowledge and skills people are expected to possess at different stages. In contrast, a process curriculum has more general aspirations such as the eradication of racism or the encouragement of autonomy. When working in this way we do not specify the outcome tightly beforehand.

Once the aims have been identified, the process curriculum needs a set of principles to handle:

- Planning, for example, how to select and organize content.

- The study and evaluation of the process.[40]

These help educators to think about what the best way of working might be. They provide a framework for making decisions about content and method. So, for example, a group of workers in a play centre may want to question gender stereotyping. To begin the process they may involve the children in a game followed by a discussion. At the outset the workers will be uncertain as to what sense the

---

[40] Lawrence Stenhouse (1975) *An Introduction to Curriculum Research and Development*, London: Heinemann, page 5. See, also, Alistair Ross (2000) *Curriculum: Construction and critique*, London: RoutledgeFalmer.

children will make of the experience and the sorts of points that may come out in discussion. Their skill lies in choosing the game, handling the discussion and in drawing out learning. One of the principles involved will be that any activity stimulates discussion about the topic and encourages collaborative learning. Judgements can be made about the process: How did people work together? What did they learn from the experience? How should we proceed? It might be that the bulk of the discussion was not about gender stereotyping, but concerned the way in which the older children accessed the most popular toys. Within a process framework this opportunity for learning would then be welcomed and exploited. A new way of approaching the original topic would have to be unearthed for a future session. In other words, the concern is also to work with what people bring to encounters.

Today, a process approach to curriculum is largely encountered in those settings where attendance is voluntary (for example, within options in schools or in activities in community and youth centres). It cannot coexist with the sort of rigidity found in national curriculum areas. However, there are still problems for informal educators here. To use a curriculum is still to specify in advance of the encounter what we are setting out to do. It entails structuring and managing encounters to match the aims of the educator (and sometimes the participants).

The process of informal education

At the centre of our work as informal educators is interaction or conversation - and in conversation everything is so unpredictable. Talk can lead anywhere. In this sense it is difficult to be specific about outcome or aim. Content certainly cannot be sequenced in any meaningful way beforehand. Imagine yourself entering a classroom as an educator. Often the conversation of students will fade and they will turn to look to the front and you. They will be usually waiting for you to take the lead. Indeed, they may be irritated if you did not do so. Compare this with joining a group of residents in a community lounge. Our presence may be acknowledged; it may not. It could be that the conversation turns to something that involves us. Equally we may find ourselves on the fringe awaiting a suitable opportunity to engage with the group. We are far less likely to be the centre of attention. In such settings we cannot carry a curriculum with us and hope to employ it (or impose it). We may be working with the residents association around their attempts to develop communal provision. There may be questions or issues that we would like to discuss – but we are dependent on the twists and turns of the conversation to see if we can or whether we still want to introduce them.

Informal education is, thus, not curriculum-based. It is driven by conversation and informed by certain values and commitments. This means that informal educators have constantly to be thinking about their actions and the situations they encounter. They have to balance meeting competing demands and learn to allow conversation to develop and to engage in such ways that express the values that underpin their work. (We will be exploring this in more detail in the next chapter.)

So what elements make up the informal education process? In *Figure 5.3* we set out some key dimensions to begin our exploration.

Figure 5.3: The process of informal education

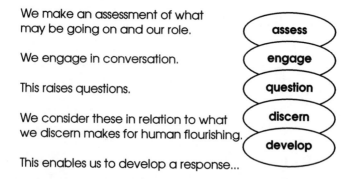

We make an assessment of what may be going on and our role. **assess**

We engage in conversation. **engage**

This raises questions. **question**

We consider these in relation to what we discern makes for human flourishing. **discern**

This enables us to develop a response... **develop**

As *Figure 5.3* shows, rather than using a curriculum we are guided in our actions by an understanding of our role as educators and certain commitments. These commitments should be related to our ideas about what may make for human flourishing. In earlier chapters, which looked at conversation and fostering democracy, we noted some of these. They include having a concern for, and respecting others; being committed to the search for truth and wisdom; and working to extend democracy.

Three crucial aspects are implicit in *Figure 5.3*. Each of the dimensions involves action, reflection and learning. They are present throughout. If we return to the example of the residents in the community lounge, we as educators have to make an initial assessment of what might be going on and our role. This means making decisions about how to act in a way that is appropriate. It might include thinking about where to sit, who to make eye contact with, and what to (or not) say. In other words, we have to reflect as we act. We may well be walking towards the group as we make these decisions. From the onset we will be seeking to learn – about them, the setting and our role. As we learn we will, at the same time, be looking to foster the learning of others. Our role as educator does not begin here when we open our mouths. The people we appear to be – our dress, demeanour and deeds will 'speak' before we do.

Figure 5.4: The practice of informal education

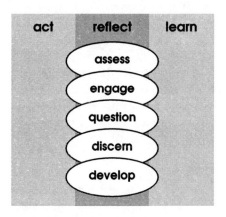

As we have seen, we often make decisions 'on our feet' about how we should act and which direction to take. For informal educators, time is not usually divided up like lessons or periods. Even work sessions are not neatly bounded. Moving from an assessment to a response may sometimes take days or weeks with educators spending a lot of time thinking about what has happened or been said. On the other hand it may occur in an instant. This is not a neat step-by-step process. As we saw with regard to thinking, elements interact and connect in ways which create highly variable timescales. Like conversation itself, the process ebbs and flows. People will want to revisit issues and topics: they will tend to want to move at their own pace. Informal educators have to learn to live with this.

The sorts of questions that may be raised in encounters will vary - but some at least will relate to our impression of what may be going on for the other people involved. In this sense, informal educators are concerned with outcomes. We will be on the look out for changes in others (as well as ourselves). However, this is not our prime orientation - we look for change, but do so knowing that it can be very difficult to recognize; and that the results of informal education often take some time to surface. Sometimes the result may be inaction rather than action. For example, a conversation with an informal educator about the demands of studying may persuade a person to embark on a course of study. Equally it may convince a third person listening to abandon a part-time course and concentrate on their job. It may make you, the educator, reflect on your attitude towards your own child who is studying for their final school examinations, and change your behaviour as a parent. Such outcomes could be neither predicted at the start of the conversation; nor can they be measured properly as outputs. (We return to this in Chapter 6.)

In conclusion

Some people still talk of such things as the 'informal education curriculum'. This is partly borne of confusing informal education with the idea of a negotiated-curriculum. The latter entails educators and the learners sitting down in advance and working out what the curriculum will be. We might do this when, for example, planning a residential experience. Such planning may well arise out of a conversation - but it is not to be confused with conversation. Informal educators may wrongly see the creation of a curriculum as a means of offering status and stability to their work. Where a national curriculum exists for schools it is tempting to imagine that what is essential for formal educational settings is also needed for the informal. In fact this subverts informal education - it is the very absence of curriculum that is a key defining feature.

A further mistake some people can make is to overlook the fact that educators use a range of approaches. Here we need to repeat a point. Informal educators can and must employ more formal approaches from time to time. We will work along the line from a to c in *Figure 5.5*.

Figure 5.5: Conversation and curriculum

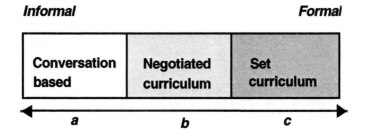

If we go back to the street workers mentioned in Chapter 1 we can see the mix. Much of their work will be of the conversation variety (*a*), but they will also be running small projects and groups, perhaps organizing residentials (*b*). Here they may sit down with those involved and talk through the programme. They decide together what they will do - they negotiate a curriculum. Our workers may also be interested in water-sports. Here they may well organize a course on safety - where they decide the content and the process (*c*). Again, we need to emphasize that what we are calling informal educators are those that tend to work in the area of (a), but who will also make use of (*b*) and (*c*). Educators who mostly operate around (b) could be labelled non-formal educators because of their interest in 'bottom-up' or negotiated curriculum building.

All educators have to attend to process but informal educators have far greater leeway to engage with it. For many formal educators questions of process are increasingly determined by others. In initiatives such as literacy and numeracy hours, schoolteachers are told both what to teach and how to teach. If others control content, they will inevitably secure a hold over the process – certain things, it seems, can only be taught in certain ways. Equally, those who control the process acquire a powerful influence over content. The message for informal educators is clear. If either of these is determined by parties outside the dialogical process then workers will be in danger of being transformed into a formal educators.

Some questions to consider

1. There will probably be aspects of your work that are more product-oriented, others process oriented. Review your work - see what fits where.

2. Are there particular reasons or pressures that these pieces of work are oriented the way they are? Are there changes that you want to make?

3. Consider a recent example of your work. In what ways did you act, reflect and learn?

4. In what areas of your work, if any, do you use a curriculum? Would you describe it as a product or a process approach?

Follow up

There are several things you can do to deepen your exploration of working with process.

Visit the 'working with process' support page at www.infed.org/foundations for further discussion, examples, activities and links.

Read Mary Crosby (2001) 'Working with people as an informal educator' in Linda Deer Richardson and Mary Wolfe (eds.) (2001) *The Principles and Practice of Informal Education*, London: RoutledgeFalmer, pages 54-61.

Read Allan Brown's review of programme and process in (1992) *Groupwork*, Aldershot: Arena, pages 96-130. This piece provides an overview of some fairly common ways of thinking about working with process in groups.

Read Parker J. Palmer (1998) *The Courage To Teach. Exploring the inner landscape of a teacher's life*, San Francisco: Jossey-Bass Publishers. A moving exploration of the 'true spirit' of teaching.

Chapter 6

Evaluating practice

In Chapter One we argued that informal education is future orientated, concerned with development and growth. Therefore, as educators we must foster learning that aids this. Looking towards the future and planning is vital but this must take place alongside reflection on what has happened. If we are concerned about the quality and effectiveness of our practice we must constantly reflect upon and monitor our work. That means asking questions such as 'Am I doing this right?' 'Did what I say help or hinder learning?' 'Why did today seem a success but last night so flat?' 'Why is X being driven from the group, and should I do something about it?' Questions such as these constantly occur to a good practitioner. They arise before, after, and during every session.

Usually we 'discuss' such questions with ourselves (with or without moving our lips!) Often we talk them through with colleagues, friends and partners. These conversations on the phone or face-to-face may seem casual and unfocussed but they are vital. They are a means by which we evaluate and make sense of our work. Wise educators will take care to cultivate a network of people with whom they can share their work. Some will understand informal education and can contribute to the process of evaluation from a shared perspective. Others may offer valuable insights based on their work in other settings and traditions. All will need to be trustworthy – people with whom serious as well as trivial concerns can be shared. No one can, or should, create such a network for us. It is our responsibility to establish our own.

Asking and answering questions like those mentioned earlier is what evaluation is about. It is something that is going on all the time and should not be just a one-off event. We monitor what is happening, as it is happening. In other words, we reflect as we work. This involves evaluation - making judgements and putting a value on things. As a result, we are able to respond in more appropriate ways to situations.

Evaluation, in its original Latin sense, meant to strengthen. In recent years, evaluation has often come to mean something else. It has become a tool of funders wanting to judge what is 'successful', what 'works' and what should or should not be invested in. Rather than being an integral part of educating, this type of evaluation is more concerned with counting and comparing. Such approaches are usually enforced from outside. Their implementation is entrusted to imported consultants - men and women employed to tell others whether what they are doing is right or wrong. It is an approach that takes little or no account of the ongoing evaluation that is intrinsic to conversation. It also changes the nature of the questions, and usually appeals to different values and interests. This is why we must always ask whose values and judgements shape the questions being asked? In this short chapter we want to explore what evaluation is appropriate for informal educators.

Three approaches to evaluation

Three broad approaches to evaluation are commonly found within informal education practice. Educators will often have to work with all three.

Directed evaluation. In this approach external agents, often funders, set criteria. The focus is largely upon measurable outcomes and outputs. It is chiefly used as a tool of management and control. Comparisons are made between agencies and workers. The methods used are designed to measure 'efficiency', 'effectiveness' and 'value for money'. The result is often the creation of conformity as agencies and workers strive to 'deliver' the required outputs and outcomes. It also fuels competition, the fabrication of results, and the rejection of 'unprofitable customers' in order to sustain funding. Examples of this approach are commonplace in education and health services. Some of the most visible signs of its use are league tables, funding report forms and inspection reports.

Negotiated evaluation. Here the judgements regarding practice are made according to criteria agreed between the different parties involved. Management committees, funders, workers and participants may all make some contribution to deciding what is to be evaluated and how. There is debate and discussion, although not all may be involved in everything. The criteria and the method are not imposed by outside bodies and can vary from situation to situation. However, they are set out in advance. The methods can be close to those used in directed evaluation. Apart from collecting data (about, for example, the number of people using a facility) this approach commonly involves evaluation forms and questionnaires.

Dialogical evaluation. This approach places the responsibility for evaluation on educators and participants. Its purpose is to enrich practice and it is part and parcel of practice. We seek conversations that focus on issues concerning the value of people's experiences and learning. This entails engaging with people to describe experiences, explore meanings, confront issues, and reconstruct practice.[41] As part of the daily round of working, we encourage people to look at what they have learnt and their experiences of learning. We listen to what they are saying (and not saying) and also reflect upon our own experiences. We ask questions or make suggestions so that people may develop their abilities to evaluate their own experiences. At the same time we may invite them to join with us in making judgements about the work. For much of this time this is not

---

[41] John Smyth (1993) *Teachers as Collaborative Learners*, Buckingham: Open University Press.

planned and does not make use of formal tools. It twists and develops through conversation. This means it can take some unravelling – and hence the place for recording and exploring things with others. More formal activities are also often necessary to stimulate reflection. These can range from the production of annual reports, through things like focus groups, to residentials and business meetings. The keynotes are dialogue and the exercise of democratic power. This approach involves the making of decisions by those directly involved (and who also have to live with the consequences of their actions).

The timing of evaluation is significant. Evaluations undertaken during the lifetime of a project or a piece of work are often described as formative. Their purpose is to help make decisions about our next step or strategy. This contrasts with evaluations taking place on completion of pieces of work. These are often called summative. They look back and review what has been done; they literally 'sum up'. Such evaluation is often required by funders and linked to whether targets have been met. In practice both forms of evaluation can run together - a summative judgement being used to plan new work.

Problems in evaluating informal education

In recent years informal educators have been put under great pressure to provide 'output indicators', 'qualitative criteria', 'objective success measures' and 'adequate assessment criteria'. Those working with young people have been encouraged to show how young people have developed 'personally and socially through participation'.[42] As we shall see, the forms of evaluation used in the formal

---

[42] Questions raised in this section are discussed at greater length in Tony Jeffs and Mark K. Smith (1999) 'Informal education and health promotion' in E. R. Perkins, I. Simnett and L. Wright (eds.) *Evidence-Based Health Promotion*, Chichester: John Wiley. The quote is from OFSTED (1997) *The Contribution of Youth Services to Drug Education*, London: Stationery Office.

education sector and in most other areas pose problems for informal educators.

First, the different things that influence the way people behave can't be easily broken down. For example, an informal educator working with a project to reduce teen crime on two estates might notice that the one with a youth club open every weekday evening has less crime than the estate without such provision. But what will this variation, if it even exists, prove? It could equally be explained by differences in the ethos of local schools, policing practices, housing, unemployment rates, and the willingness of people to report offences.

Second, those who may have been affected by the work of informal educators are often not easily identified. It may be possible to list those who have been worked with directly over a period of time. However, much contact is sporadic and may even take the form of a single encounter. The indirect impact is just about impossible to quantify. Our efforts may result in significant changes in the lives of people we do not work with. This can happen as those we work with directly develop. Consider, for example, how we reflect on conversations that others recount to us, or ideas that we acquire second- or third-hand. Good informal education aims to achieve a ripple effect. We hope to encourage learning through conversation and example and can only have a limited idea of what the true outcome might be.

Third, change can rarely be monitored even on an individual basis. For example, informal educators who focus on alcohol abuse within a particular group can face an insurmountable problem if challenged to provide evidence of success. They will not be able to measure use levels prior to intervention, during contact or subsequent to the completion of their work. In the end all the educator will be able to offer, at best, is vague evidence relating to contact or anecdotal material.

Fourth, there is an issue with timescales. Change of the sort with which informal educators are concerned does not happen overnight. Changes in values, and the ways that people come to appreciate themselves and others, are notoriously hard to identify - especially as they are happening. What may seem ordinary at the time can, with hindsight, be recognized as special.

Last, we encounter the thorny topic of candour within evaluation. The growth of the audit culture with its concern that everything public servants do must be measured and assessed to ensure 'value for money' has created a cascade of forms and returns. These accumulate information regarding how we spend our time, where we go, who we meet and what we do. The justification for all this bureaucracy is that it rewards success and penalises failure, identifies 'good practice' and encourages efficiency. Whether it actually does these things is another question. It certainly costs a great deal in terms of the time and effort of face-to-face workers. For example a detached youth work project studied by one of the writers now allows 30 minutes out of each two and a half hour session for workers to complete the required returns. That is in addition to the time set aside for staff to discuss amongst themselves how the session went. Bureaucracy consumes 20 per cent of the part-time staff budget. The same project had two full-time workers and a four-day a week administrator who only handled returns, funding applications and other paper work. It was estimated less than half the full-time staffing budget 'funded' face-to-face contact time.

In tandem with the audit culture we have the escalating use by funders of payment-by-results. This demands that informal educators 'deliver' measured outcomes as a condition of payment. Community centre users must be pressurised into completing NVQs of dubious value; youth club members Youth Achievement Awards; and parents popping into the children's or parents' centre must prove they come from a deprived area if the funding targets are to be achieved. So "where do you live?" not "would you like a cup of tea?" becomes the must-ask opening gambit. Of course much of this counting and measuring has little to do with 'value for money' or generating efficiency. Rather it justifies a top-heavy management layer, teaches the minions to 'know their place' and cultivates a climate of fear that ensures compliance with instructions from 'up-the-line'.

Inevitably, as all parties are aware but many cannot admit, this leads to dishonesty. Money, unchallenged, will leech out all other values unless we are alert to the danger - and we are not taking sufficient care to ensure that does not occur. A conspiracy of silence pervades the sector. Just as many schools fiddle their SATs and attendance returns to improve their league table positions, so informal educators are tempted to tweak the evaluation process to protect their funding and keep the inspectors happy.

The evaluation and audit culture is a canker, propagating dishonesty and punishing the honest. It erodes the self-respect of practitioners and corrodes our relationship with those we seek to work with. They are not so stupid as to be unaware they are being manipulated and managed to attain externally imposed outcomes and outputs - outcomes they never consented to and care not a fig for. They also learn that when measured outcomes are the order of the day conversation, argument and debate become viewed as a risky diversion. Discussion is to be avoided as it diverts the staff's attention from what has become their central task - achieving a good score, a high rating. The audit culture and the payment by results regime actively discourage the unplanned and spontaneous. They are intolerant of autonomy and what cannot be measured. They worm their way into the sphere of informal relationships and stimulate a disposition towards conformity and passivity.

So how can informal education be evaluated?

Because evaluation is difficult does not mean we should ignore or avoid it. Rather we must find ways of evaluating our work that are compatible with our values and concern to foster democracy and association. This inevitably means that dialogue and conversation will be at the heart of our evaluative efforts.

As well as considering the methods, we also need to be thinking about what is to be evaluated. Here we might be asking questions about:

- **Interactions**. What are the characteristics of these? What purposes did they serve? What initiated them? To what extent were they educative? Are they sustained? Do they reflect the sort of values we are seeking to encourage?

- **Focus**. What issues and topics form the focus for conversation? Which of these are initiated by us, and which by others? What are the most common subjects or concerns?

- **Setting**. Where is the work undertaken? What physical settings best stimulate conversation? What is the impact of the setting upon subject matter, the nature of those worked with, and the quality of interaction?

- **Aims**. What were we as educators aiming to achieve? What were the aims of others? Were there conflicts between the two?

- **Strategies**. How did we, as educators, plan to achieve our aims? Who set these? What moves did we make? How, if at all, were they altered and who influenced this? What strategies did others have? How did they change?

- **Outcomes**. Were outcomes set, and if so by whom? What appeared to be the outcome for different participants? What did we learn from our engagement? Are there issues and questions we need to address? Who needs to know about these?

By considering these - and how they relate to each other - we can begin to judge or value events and experiences. We do this by looking to our understanding of what makes for human flourishing and our role (see *Figure 5.3*). We then have some basis upon which to make decisions about our next step or to plan strategies.

The above discussion focuses on the dialogue between participants and educators. It places these at the centre of the evaluation. There are, however, third parties that may be interested in the outcome of any evaluation – funders, managers and inspectors. Although we would argue it is inappropriate for dialogical evaluation to be tailored to meet their expectations (this would warp the process), educators should be mindful of these. Therefore, it may necessary for educators to undertake parallel evaluations that supply the 'evidence' funders and others require. In this way, educators may be involved in dialogical, negotiated and directed evaluations at the same time.

In conclusion

For educators the primary interest should always be the quality of the learning experience and how it may enhance, or inhibit, well-being. Evaluation is part of everyday practice and helps us to sustain our focus. It is not the mere counting and measuring of things, but involves the difficult task of valuing. We have to make judgements about the 'rightness' of actions.

Some questions to consider

1. What do you do to evaluate your work? What do others do to evaluate your work? Are these compatible?

2. Can you think of ways in which statistics might be collected with regard to your work which would tell you and others what you are doing?

3. 'All you do is stand around and natter', says a friend who regularly collects you from work. How might you produce evidence to show that this is not all that you do?

Follow up

There are several things you can do to deepen your exploration of evaluating practice.

Visit the 'evaluating practice' support page at www.infed.org/foundations for further discussion, examples, activities and links.

Read Angela Everitt and Pauline Hardiker's chapter 'The purposes of evaluation' in their (1996) book *Evaluating for Good Practice*, London: Macmillan, pages 19-36. The book explores a critical approach to evaluation.

Read E. Leslie Sewell (1966) *Looking at Youth Clubs*, London: National Association of Youth Clubs. A classic pamphlet exploring how to make judgements about youth work. Available online via the support page.

Read Marie Paneth (1944) *Branch Street: A Sociological Study*, London: George Allen and Unwin. This wonderful account of an action-research project undertaken with young people in a poor London neighbourhood can be read as an almost perfect example of evaluation-in-practice. Paneth continually reflects on her work and relationships with colleagues, the community and the young people with whom she works. Find out more about Paneth and 'Branch Street' on the support page.

Chapter 7

Living with values

Informal education is a moral craft. Because we are concerned with fostering learning in life, as it is lived, we often have to make difficult choices. The people we are, and the values we hold, are fundamental to how we deal with these and how we are experienced. As Parker J. Palmer has argued, our work flows from our character and integrity.[43] The complex personal and social choices others, and we, make are not external to our work but sit at the very heart of it.

Core values

On what basis do we make choices about our practice? As we have already seen informal educators should be guided by certain commitments. On the one hand are found what we can call 'core values' – a set of beliefs that are shared and debated among informal educators. On the other, are our personal commitments and values. At times these will coincide, and at others they will clash. We have to make choices around each of these sets of values and live with and by them. Informal educators do not have a ready-made set

---

[43] Parker J. Palmer (1998) *The Courage To Teach, Exploring The Inner Landscape Of A Teacher's Life*, San Francisco, California: Jossey-Bass Inc. Publishers.

of guidelines telling them what is right and wrong. They can't have this and hope to continue to engage honestly with the everyday experiences of those they work with. They have to make up their own minds as they encounter different situations. This they do in conversation – with others, the core values and themselves.

Let us begin by thinking about what some of the core or first order values may be.

- **Respect for persons**. This requires us to recognize the dignity and uniqueness of every human being. It also entails behaving in ways that convey that respect. This means, for example, that we avoid exploiting people for our, or others', ends.

- **The promotion of well-being**. We must work for the welfare of all. We must further human flourishing. That means, for example, we must always try to avoid causing harm, and seek to enhance the well-being of others.

- **Truth**. Perhaps the first duty of the educator is to truth. This means that we must not teach or embrace something we know or believe to be false. We must search for truth and be open in dialogue to the truth in what others say. However, we should not be fearful of confronting falsehood where we find it.

- **Democracy**. Democracy involves the belief that all human beings ought to enjoy the chance of self-government or autonomy. Implicit in this is the idea that all are equal citizens. A fundamental purpose of informal education is to foster democracy through experiencing it. We must seek within our practice to offer opportunities for people to enjoy and exercise democratic rights.

- **Fairness and equality**. Informal educators have a responsibility to work for relationships characterized by fairness. Any discrimination has to be justified on the basis it will lead to greater equity. We must also look to promote equality. Actions must be evaluated with regard to the way people are treated, the opportunities open to them, and the rewards they receive.

These values are difficult to define and are often argued about. As an example will show later in this chapter, it is often difficult to see how we can distribute resources in a fair and equitable way. Similar problems can occur with all the above. We can soon find ourselves having to work through various conflicts. For example, there might be clash between a commitment to democracy and the promotion of well-being. A community group are approached and offered money for new play equipment by the makers of a docu-soap. The programme makers want access to their meetings and to focus on the daily lives of the members. The committee has voted in favour of the venture. As educators, we may know that there is significant possibility of the material being misused, the estate being labelled, and there being harm done to some of the individuals involved. Do we prioritize the protection of vulnerable members, by seeking to reverse the decision? If this fails would we go behind the backs of the group to the owners of the community building (in this case the council) and use our influence to persuade them not to grant permission for filming? Do we simply allow the filming to proceed and work with the consequences? Clashes such as these are tricky to deal with. Also, we can all envisage examples involving deeply held religious, political and personal views that can be very difficult to resolve for agencies and educators.

Ethical judgements are always being made and justified. In conversation others can demand to know 'why did you do that?' and 'why did you say that?' Educators need a set of values to inform and shape their work - otherwise they will be rudderless.

Moral authority

Educators must, Colin Wringe says, constantly review their practices. This is to ensure we do not behave in unjust ways or help create injustice in the future. He reminds us we are 'no more entitled to pursue policies which lead to injustice than the police or... Health Service'.[44]

Aims are not spelt out on a daily basis. Would anything be more likely to alienate those we work with than constantly proclaiming 'I am here to do good, you know', or informing those within earshot that 'my mission is to help you'. Some things are best left unsaid, better conveyed by actions and behaviour. However, just as doctors are taught the properties of drugs to cure their patients - so informal educators gain skills to make a positive contribution towards the betterment of individuals, groups and communities. Therefore, for example, knowledge, like time, must not be shared indiscriminately. Judgements are needed about how it is to be employed and who, if anyone, will benefit. A worker, for example, would not be expected to give the address of the local refuge to an abusive husband seeking his wife, because they know it might put her and others at risk. Nor would a youth worker pass on the phone number of a known drug dealer to a young person without carefully reflecting on the motives of those who are asking.

Few informal educators can be unaware that people learn from their example. Our behaviour, attitudes and values will be scrutinised by those we work with and for. There will be those seeking a role model and others straining to detect hypocrisy. Informal educators are pressured to step-in whenever they encounter unacceptable behaviour. It is not easy for us to overlook such things as bullying or intolerance. People can look to us to set boundaries, to draw the line between acceptable and unacceptable behaviour. This means we must learn, for instance, how to indicate disapproval towards say racist or sexist language without being seen as prigs or killjoys. We, therefore, need a repertoire of techniques so we may influence people without alienating them. This is easier said than done. It can demand great skill, and sometimes courage, to sustain dialogue

---

[44] Colin Wringe (1988) *Understanding Educational Aims*, London: Unwin Hyman, page 101.

without sanctioning unacceptable views or behaviour; to remain in a group yet apart from it.

Those we work with may at times make fun of certain values such as honesty, reliability or selflessness. That said, informal educators are expected to be fair, truthful, punctilious about fulfilling obligations, and thoughtful and unselfish in their conduct. However great the temptation to go with the moral flow we really have no choice. We must aspire to embody such values because our right 'to be listened to' largely flows from this. It does not necessarily come from our having superior knowledge. The way we conduct ourselves, and the care we take with people, are recognized. Gradually, we may come to be seen as people who can be trusted, have integrity and are wise. It is qualities such as these that allow us to play a part in people's lives. They give us a chance to deepen learning opportunities for others in different situations, and to ask questions about what might be good or bad. In other words, they underpin and express our 'moral authority'. Those who possess them gain a capacity to influence situations and to prompt people to think of their, and others, well-being.

If we are heeded it is mainly because people see us as deserving of respect. If we are not then people will ask why should they listen to us; why should our example be followed; and even why bother to engage in conversation with us? It goes without saying that an obese health educator who smokes, props up the bar most nights and avoids physical activity will not find their homilies regarding what to eat or drink given due attention. Neither will those seeking to challenge values and attitudes get far unless they monitor their own behaviour to avoid inconsistencies and double standards. Mission statements on the wall about equality will count for little if people observe us treating secretaries like dogs-bodies and caretakers as skivvies. Attention to our own actions is crucial.

High moral tone is not in itself sufficient. Knowledge, personality and attitude will always count for a great deal. We have to be wise. This is something that is expressed in action. It is not a thing that goes with the job, acquired with the keys to the filing cabinet. We see wisdom in sound judgements, for example regarding our behaviour and our choice of ends and means. Unlike many of those working in formal settings, contact with informal educators will usually be on a voluntary basis. People are rarely under any obligation to talk with an informal educator. We must be well-informed, challenging and culturally aware. Without something worthwhile to say, something more than common sense, people are unlikely to benefit from prolonged contact. Also, given the voluntary nature of our encounters we, even more than other teachers, must be lively, enthusiastic and amusing. Who after all would willingly spend time with a humourless, pessimistic bore? However, we are not companion horses but educators. We cannot sacrifice moral authority for popularity.

Unlike schoolteachers we have no national curriculum to fall back on, no examinations holding a promise of employment. We have nothing to sustain a learning relationship after indifference, even loathing, has supplanted respect. Thus, moral authority – being seen by others as people with integrity, wisdom and an understanding of right and wrong - is something we must seek and preserve.

Making choices

As informal educators we are always making choices. Having to decide such things as who to work with, where to operate and how to allocate our time. In part managers may make such decisions for us. They may identify the needs to be met and tasks to be undertaken. However, we still retain leeway as to what to prioritize and how to spend our time. Because it is difficult to supervise informal education, guidelines are usually vague. Workers may be employed to run a project, support a community initiative or promote a specific activity, but their remit will almost always allow some freedom to decide how they operate. It will be up to the workers to select which individuals or groups to focus upon, respond to positively, or to ignore or avoid.

Here we run into problems. We may fancy working with young men rather than young women; feel uncomfortable with people of a different 'race'; or 'get a special buzz' from spending time with those who share similar interests. For obvious reasons we may be reluctant to own up to this. It can smack of self-interest and prejudice. It may generate harsh criticism. These are matters we need to explore. We may not even be aware of what we are doing or of whose interests we are putting first. One of the dilemmas we face as informal educators is that for the most part we have only ourselves as a resource. We have to play to our strengths. If we enjoy drama then there may be great benefits using that medium. However, this requires a special concern to avoid indulgence. Our first duty is to the needs of 'participants' or clients'. Many workers fall out when one party believes the other is using the job to indulge their enthusiasms, or is putting their interests above those of participants. Such behaviour is rightly seen as unacceptable.

Once we are clear about putting participants first we have to make judgements about need. We have to decide what work will create the best opportunities for people to share in a common life. Unfortunately these two criteria - benefit and need - rarely coincide. Imagine for a moment a group of young people in a deprived inner-city locality with whom you have been in touch for a number of years. Amongst them is a bright articulate young woman with a lively interest in, and special talent for, music. With encouragement and support it is possible she may achieve a great deal, go to university and make a career for herself out of music. Not only may she benefit, but so will the wider community as a consequence of her becoming a positive role model for other young people. Recently she has become discouraged, beginning to think college and a musical career are 'beyond the likes of her'. You sense now is the time for a concerted effort. Your support, encouragement and practical help will probably make a difference.

In the same circle is a young man already involved in petty crime, with no discernible interests apart from 'mucking about and drugs'. Like his older brother before him, he is drifting away from the group. Unreliable, often aggressive, frequently uncommunicative he is neither popular nor respected. Everyone - teachers, social workers, parents and most of his peers - has given up on him. Each has decided the die is cast and the question is not will he get into trouble with the law, but how serious will it be. You, however, believe that maybe, just maybe, with some focused work it might be possible keep him out of serious trouble, at least for the time being. By building upon your past relationship, and showing that at least one person cares, something might be achieved. Your dilemma is which of the two to prioritize. Focusing on the young man who is clearly the most deprived of the two would not be a popular decision, neither is it necessarily likely to be the most productive in terms of 'outcomes'. Concentrate on the young woman and public, tangible benefits are likely to accrue for her, the group and wider community.

No off-the-peg formula or checklist exists capable of providing an answer to this or similar dilemmas. We must choose according to the circumstances. As Eduard Lindeman reminds us 'values arise out of the social process'[45]. However, we must always be aware that those we work with, or for, may ask us to justify our decision. We need to demonstrate we made an ethical judgement, a decision based upon notions of the right conduct (and not upon our likes and dislikes, or self-interest).

What we consider to be the right conduct may not accord with our manager's views, or with the opinion of other interested parties. Working in ways that honour core values can place us in difficult, even dangerous, positions. We know of people being sacked because they placed their duty to a 'client' above agency procedures; physically attacked because their actions were seen to undermine the position of a group in a community; and cold-shouldered by colleagues because they 'blew the whistle' on the unprofessional conduct of one of their co-workers. Fear around such matters can lead us into compromising core values. We may look for the easy way out. Unfortunately, there often isn't a solution that is both comfortable and honourable. Ducking difficult

---

[45] Eduard Lindeman (1926) *The Meaning of Adult Education* 3e, Norman, Ok.: University of Oklahoma, p. 101.

questions undermines our moral authority. We need to demonstrate that we are making an ethical judgement.

There are some obvious steps we could be taking. First, we should be exploring questions with colleagues. Core values are shared and debated in communities of practice. It is important that we can place our ideas and actions in relation to the main currents within that community. We might ask 'What would other play (or community, youth or community education) workers think about this?' Second, we need to know where the boundaries are. What are our employers' expectations? What is acceptable within this community or that? It is through unthinking action that these are often transgressed. Third, we need to gain some protection through membership of a union and professional association. However, such actions can only take us so far. Our first concern should be to do what is good and right, not what is 'correct'. We need the courage to break rules and be ready to be called to account for this.

Codes of ethics and codes of practice

When we are faced with making difficult decisions how can we order our thinking? Should we have a code of ethics setting out moral guidelines or a code of practice that seeks to regulate behaviour? The American philosopher John Rawls has argued that we should act on the basis that we do not know whether we will be the one who gains or loses by the choice made[46]. This means we should treat others as we ourselves would expect to be treated. Thinking such as this provides the basis for most codes of practice or ethics adopted by professions such as social workers, medical practitioners and journalists.

These codes seek to create a common basis upon which the relationship between the worker and the 'client' will be founded. Informal educators do not have their own code of practice or ethics at present (although a number of

---

[46] John Rawls (1971) *A Theory of Justice*, Cambridge, Mass.: Harvard University Press.

organizations are seeking to create them for youth workers and others). Many of those we work alongside do have such codes, but how significant a part they play in shaping their daily practice is often difficult to judge. Codes can be difficult to apply. Sarah Banks reminds us that social workers, for example, have 'different layers of duties which may conflict with each other'[47]. The potentially competing duties she identifies are to:

- users;

- colleagues and the profession;

- the agency and employer; and

- society.

Rarely are these cohesive. Groups of users or colleagues, for example, rarely speak with one voice. Conflict amongst colleagues or users is often what makes our job most difficult. Nor are all these compatible. For example, we might identify a group of young people truanting from the school to which we are attached. We judge that they have educational and social needs that we can meet as informal educators. Colleagues within the school may not want this group in the school as some of them have been excluded in the past for violent behaviour. They would like you to leave the group alone. Your employer - the school - considers that your responsibility should be primarily to those who attend and engage with the school. The head, like many in the local community, see what you are doing with the truants as 'giving treats to bad boys and girls' at the expense of other young people from equally deprived backgrounds. Here is a typical example of the sort of conflict that can arise. Whose wishes should we prioritize – those of our employer, colleagues, members of the local community or the potential participants in our work. And if we say 'participants' are we talking about the small group of 'troublemakers' or the

47 Sarah Banks (2001) *Ethics and Values in Social Work*, London: Palgrave, page 122.

remainder of young people who are 'good' students? Having answered that question would our response be different if some of the truants expressed a wish to have a working relationship with us?

Perhaps the strongest case for codes relates to the need to establish what is and what is not acceptable behaviour between workers and those they engage with. Clarke and Asquith summarise the type of rules which 'govern' the relationship between a social worker and their client.[48] These would have to be adjusted for informal educators, but in many respects they are applicable. The clients' rights are summarized as follows. To:

1. be treated as an end i.e. that their interests are placed above those of the agency and the worker;

2. self-determination;

3. be accepted for what one is, and not encounter an attitude of condemnation;

4. be treated as a unique individual and not merely as belonging to a certain category;

5. non-discrimination on irrelevant grounds, such as 'race';

6. treatment on the principles of honesty, openness and non-deception;

7. have information given to the worker treated as confidential;

8. a professionally competent service;

9. access to resources for which there exists an entitlement.

Perhaps the big difficulty in transferring this to the world of informal education is that unlike, for example, social workers, lawyers or therapists we cannot identify a single 'client'. Working with groups and communities, engaging in conversation creates difficulties regarding questions of

---

[48] C. Clarke with S. Asquith (1985) *Social Work and Social Philosophy*, London: Routledge and Kegan Paul, page 29.

confidentiality and access to resources. Yet the right to self-determination, protection against discrimination and to be treated as an end are clearly applicable to both the individuals and groups we work with.

A benefit of a code of ethics is that we, from the onset, would have to take account of the ethical dimensions of our work. It would provide a set of boundaries, a basis for professional debate and judgement. For example, questions as to whether someone has acted unprofessionally can then be measured against agreed criteria. The downside is that the benefits may be more illusory than real. However that should not deter us from beginning to consider what values should or should not inform and regulate our practice. A good example of a central element of practice around which constant difficulties occur is confidentiality. We need to ask would a code of ethics help or hinder us in relation to this?

Confidentiality

We have already discussed the need for open and honest dialogue both with colleagues and with those we work with. In the next chapter we will be stressing the importance of record keeping. We now have to ask what, if any, limits must we place around the sharing of information?

As informal educators we are often told things 'in confidence'. We also see things that, if revealed, could cause problems for others. Every day we have to make decisions regarding whether to share information or suspicions. There are no hard and fast rules about this. As we have seen, educators have to go back to their core values and consider these in relation to the situation. For example, we may learn that the police are about to mount an operation to catch under-age young people buying cigarettes and alcohol. Is this information something that we should keep to ourselves or share with local shopkeepers and young people? Alternatively, we may know where stolen baby clothes are being sold at greatly reduced prices to parents, most of whom are on very low incomes. If asked by a respected community police officer about this do we tell them what we know, try to evade the question or lie to them?

Educators need to be clear about the sort of questions that they are able to discuss with different parties. There are limits on dialogue that are linked to core values such as respect for persons, minimizing harm and making judgements about well-being. People may well entrust us with secrets or sensitive information. We often have to make a decision as to whether to share that material with others. Here we can get some help from Sissela Bok. She considered on what basis workers could be justified in keeping information from people and the confidences of others. She suggests that for welfare workers confidentiality can be justified on the basis of four principles:

- Human autonomy regarding personal information.

- Respect for relationships.

- Respect for promises.

- The benefit to society and people needing help.[49]

Here we can see that there are certain questions we could ask ourselves about situations. What have we promised? What harm or good does telling others do? For example, we may know of someone who regular drives under the influence of drugs and alcohol. In fact, they may leave our office in such a state intending to drive. Is our prime responsibility to the individual or to the unknown third parties they may injure or kill?

To make these decisions we often need to talk with others. We may change details or speak in general terms to protect the people involved and us. There may be places where we can 'extend confidentiality'. Talking with someone outside the setting we can explore the details of the situation so as to explore how we may act. However, often we don't have the chance as action has to be taken straightaway. We have to discern what might lead to the greatest good.

---

[49] Sissela Bok (1989) *Lying: Moral Choice in Public and Private Life*, New York: Vintage Books.

A great deal of trouble can be avoided if we remember we are educators. Our purpose is to engage in dialogue to further learning, not to gather information or to gossip. Much of the space people need to explore issues does not require direct disclosure. Situations can be examined as general problems. People often don't need to say 'I did this..' or 'this happened to me' in order to think about their experiences. We need to act with some care in this area – after all direct disclosure could act against the interests of the individual concerned.

Where people need to go a step further and talk directly about their situation we will have to 'manage' the boundaries of the conversation. Some information we are legally obliged to pass on. Our employers may have procedures for disclosure around things like sexual abuse and underage sexual activity. As a result, we might try to stop people telling us certain things. Our possession of that knowledge might work against their well-being. We should certainly try to make people aware of the rules under which we operate so that they can judge the consequences of telling us things. In certain circumstances we may encourage people instead to talk to those who can retain a high level of confidentiality (such as counsellors and priests).

People may make sensitive disclosures in full knowledge that we will talk with others about their situation. Indeed, that is often the purpose of them telling us! However, there will be extreme cases (which occur perhaps more often than some might imagine) where we have to make decisions regarding confidentiality that mean we will risk either losing the trust of our colleagues, or those we work with. It may even mean that we have to change our job. For our work depends upon being trusted and having the courage to act according to our principles. Once a significant number of those we work with cease to 'trust' us, for whatever reason, it can become difficult, even impossible, to do our job.

In conclusion

Like all teachers, informal educators seek to make the world more intelligible for those they work with. To achieve this we share knowledge, experience and, where appropriate, offer guidance and advice. However, we always do so within some sort of moral framework. We try to make the world not only a more understandable, but also a better, place. We seek to reduce, not exacerbate, suffering and improve life-chances not damage them. We have to live with, and work by, certain values. This can lead us into various dilemmas as we try to balance the needs and requirements of one party against that of another. The way we conduct ourselves around such matters is pivotal to the way we are viewed as educators, and the chances we have to contribute to the learning of others.

Some questions to consider

1. In what ways may we indicate disapproval towards say racist or sexist language without being seen as prigs or killjoys?

2. Consider your face-to-face work. Does the way you work, the way you treat yourself and others, reflect the values central to informal education? How have you retained moral authority?

3. Reflect on a situation where you have had to make a difficult choice about who to work with - on what basis did you make your decision?

4. Do you think that a code of practice would be a help or a hindrance to developing good practice?

Follow up

There are several things you can do to deepen your exploration of living with values.

Visit the 'living with values' support page at www.infed.org/foundations for further discussion, examples, activities and links.

Read Sarah Banks (2001) 'Professional values in informal education work' in Linda Deer Richardson and Mary Wolfe (eds.) *The Principles and Practice of Informal Education*, London: RoutledgeFalmer. See, also, her (1999) edited collection *Ethical Values in Youth Work*, London: Routledge.

Read Nel Noddings (1992) *The challenge to care in schools : an alternative approach to education*, New York: Teachers College Press. 208 pages. In this highly readable book Noddings argues that the traditional organization of school studies short-changes students. They receive schooling for the head but little for the heart and soul. She explores what it might mean to be caring in education. You can read more about Nel Noddings and a piece by her on caring in education via our support page.

Chapter 8

Organizing the daily round

How does all this translate itself into our activities on Monday morning or Tuesday night? The starting point is that informal educators need to find and foster environments in which people can talk. We have two basic options. Either we go to places where people congregate, or we create a setting that will attract them to where we are located. In youth work these approaches have been traditionally separated as detached and centre-based work. To some extent there has also been a similar split between community organization and development, and community centre work. Such divisions are reflected in almost every area of welfare and have set up false dichotomies - prison versus probation, residential versus community care and so on. One of the advantages of thinking about informal education in the way we have been here is that it takes us beyond such simplistic splits.

Informal educators undertake six basic kinds of work. These can be labelled as follows[50].

- **Being about** involves activities such as walking round the area, visiting local drinking places and going into the

---

[50] Taken from Mark K. Smith (1994) *Local Education. Community, conversation, praxis*, Milton Keynes: Open University Press, Chapter 5.

school. In centres 'being about' translates into the time spent sitting round the bar, and coffee lounge. The aim, generally, is to be seen, to make and maintain contact with people, and to intervene where appropriate. This is a positive activity requiring planning and reflection. It neither a 'filler' nor something undertaken randomly.

- **Being there** involves informal educators setting time aside for responding to situations and crises. 'Being there' is a holding operation. It can involve some practical assistance. It might mean, for example, going with someone to a rights project. The other key aspect is being a 'shoulder to cry on' in times of crisis. It involves taking steps to be contactable and in a position to respond.

- **Working with individuals and groups** describes more 'formal' encounters. It is linked into ideas about the depth of work undertaken. It entails moving beyond the making and maintenance of contact, or the holding operation that often takes place when 'being there'. 'Working with' involves building an environment in which people can entertain feelings, reflect on their experiences, think about things and make plans. It entails working to deepen conversation and to further democracy. With groups, for example, our task is, on the one hand, to work for democratic mutual aid. On the other hand, it is to help people to realize their purpose.

- **Doing projects** varies from one-off pieces of work; through regular sessions over a three month or 10 month period, for instance, with a girls group; to activities like residentials or study visits. It may involve short courses, for example, for carers or around childcare. Frequently, it takes the form of a particular activity such as developing a newsletter. Such projects are planned in advance; time-limited; focused on learning; and largely arise out of the work, rather than being imported as 'good ideas'. Whilst 'working with' is conversation-based, projects tend to have a curriculum or output focus.

- **Doing 'admin' and research.** Informal educators usually have various administrative tasks to complete. These can range from simple returns dealing with pay and attendance through ordering and accounts to longer term planning and fund raising. We may also have to do small research tasks. These can be to do with the places and neighbourhoods in which we work, and the problems and issues we encounter. Classically, workers can get overrun by administrative work – especially if they work in organizations and programmes that require detailed reporting. There is also the temptation for some to do more and more administrative work as an escape from the demands of face-to-face work or as a way of gaining status.

- **Reflecting on practice** allows us to develop as workers, and to work for the best interests of clients and the community (see Chapter 4). Recording our work is a key element here -   as is exploring practice with others. As a team we may talk about what happened in a session, as individuals we may sit down with a supervisor or colleague and examine what happened and our feelings about it.

Figure 7.1: Six basic modes of work

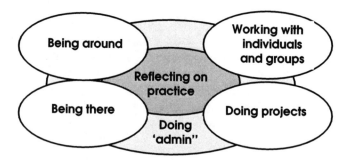

Successful practice depends on there being a good mix of these ways of working. A measure of confidence in doing them is essential for all informal educators. None are optional extras because each feeds off the other. *Figure 7.1* tries to show how these come together.

Some basic considerations

When planning our work we, thus, need to ensure that we attend to some basic points.

We work where our target groups can be found

We cannot expect people magically to come to us. For those working with young people this may mean overcoming a number of prejudices. For example, many of the places where young people can be found have not been part of the traditional youth work pattern: schools and colleges, homes and commercial leisure operations. This also involves developing new ways of getting access. Often those who manage such sites are resistant to the presence of informal educators. Our style of working can be seen as strange and threatening, not least because of the subjects we are handling. Health educators may find it difficult to work in schools and colleges, for example. These institutions often fear their presence will be interpreted as an admission that they have a problem with drugs or promiscuity. We may also want to organize new settings where we can make contact such as drop-ins, clubs and cafes.

We make ourselves and our work known

Informal educators have to work mostly in settings that are not overtly educational. As a result, we need to establish our role and be clear about what we can offer. This entails 'cold' contact work, that is to say, approaching people we have not previously met: on the street, door-to-door, or in social areas in schools and churches. Consequently, care has to be taken regarding style and manner. We have to be sensitive to the right of others to privacy; and to our own safety. We also need various 'props' to allow us to make contact: leaflets, programmes, calling cards. However, such props should reflect our priorities. Consider, for example if we have made a decision to work with older people in an area, then leaflets must be designed and prepared in a way that is sensitive to their concerns and interests.

We have a range of more organized activities into which people can feed

Informal educators need a number of projects on the go at any given time. This can help us to communicate our identity as well as offering a range of new or wanted opportunities to those we are working with. Projects can also deepen the work and give it an overt focus. For many workers it is vital they have something more to offer than conversation, and themselves. In making contact with people who are homeless it is important that they are able to offer various services, e.g. help in accessing temporary accommodation and obtaining benefits.

We have space to respond to situations

One of our key strengths is the ability to respond quickly to what people are bringing. We need to 'catch the moment'. It is important, therefore, that we do not over-programme our time. We must leave plenty of time to 'be around'. This is time that is flexible. Where crises emerge or, say, we need to spend time talking something through with a group then we can convert 'being around' to 'being there' for someone, or to 'working with'. For example, we may be working with a group of women who use a family centre drop-in. It is likely that we will have to spend time with particular individuals as issues arise - say around relationships with partners and ex-partners, income support and the educational needs of their children.

We attend to administration

Informal education is demanding and sophisticated. We can find ourselves dealing with very difficult problems, we have to work in settings that are not at all straightforward, and we have continually to think on our feet. To be clear about what we are doing we need to talk to others. We also must not underestimate the benefits of recordings, sound paper work and organization. Colleagues need to be able to cover for us if we are ill or dealing with an emergency. Activities generally involve a lot of preparation, for work to be financed applications have to be made and reports written. These areas have tended to be under-recognized. Full-time workers should be sensitive to those working part-time who are often expected to do these things unpaid and to the needs of those working on a voluntary basis.

Records and recordings are vital. However, we must ask 'what are they for?' Time spent recording is time denied from face-to-face work. Recordings have to be judged in terms of their value to practise. Three direct benefits arise. They provide us with a means to reflect on our daily practice (see Chapter 4). Through writing things down we can often see issues more clearly. For example, we may jot things down in a journal - or write a more detailed recording of an event or experience. Second, recordings allow us to plan. By looking back at what we have done - in the previous week or month - we can in turn look at what we hope to achieve. This might take the form of a list of tasks, or the concerns we face. Last, records provide for continuity. They allow us to communicate with other workers. These may be colleagues, or workers who take our place. We must always ask ourselves what would happen if we were not able to be in work tomorrow or next week? Could what we are doing be picked up, or would those we work with be left in the lurch? Records are a way of preventing us letting others down. Each may involve different types of recording, although there may be some overlap. We may keep a personal journal, recordings of specific events or experiences, and logs of work (i.e. what has happened in particular groups). The former may be more about our development, the latter may be more administrative (keeping other educators in touch with the work).

We look to our own development

If we are not learning and developing, then we are unlikely to be any good as educators. In conversation we have to be ready to change our thinking as we listen to what is said. We have to be open to the other, otherwise we are unlikely to be engaging with people in a good spirit. We must value what they have to say. Furthermore, if we are to continue to have something worthwhile to say, then we have to keep reflecting on situations and deepening our knowledge. Being wise is not a static state.

Reflection on practice is of little use unless it is informed by good theory and with a growing knowledge of the world. Reading and the exploring of ideas with others often fall by the wayside. Having trained, many rely on professional magazines and briefings in order to keep up with things. Unfortunately, these can only give a taste of policy issues and practice; they rarely give an insight into why things may be happening, or into the processes involved. Educators need to put time aside for reading and engaging with other practitioners around the issues and questions that arise around their work.

However, if this work becomes the sole focus, then narrowness can creep in. Informal educators often have enthusiasms – particular activities or interests that fascinate them. They can both bring personal satisfaction and growth, and be great assets in the work. They may be enthusiasms that could spark some of those we work with and so become tools of the work – for example, a passion for the theatre or sports. As part of the people we are they can certainly provide hooks for people to connect to us. Jokes can be made and questions asked. Our greatest resource as informal educators is 'ourselves' and we must be aware of the need to ensure we attend to maintaining the fabric of our personality and mind as much as we would a building.

Using modes as building blocks

The six modes of working provide us with the basic blocks to structure our work. In planning what we may do over a period of time we can begin by working out some rough percentages. We might even try drawing a pie chart with the various modes represented (See *Figure 7.2*).

Just how we split up these elements depends on the work we are doing. Some jobs may involve more administration, others may have a different balance between project work and being around. For example, some community development work can involve a substantial amount of letter and report writing, and keeping up with policy changes.

Elements can shade into one another when planning. We often do not know in advance when we will be needed to 'be there' for someone. Similarly, we may set time aside for working with people and they do not turn up so we can then use this space for doing paperwork.

Figure 7.2: Time allocation

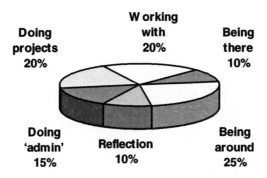

The work split featured is for a student support worker in a further education college who works half time. She plans her week so that she spends about 4 hours around the student areas - the canteen, the 'common room', etc. Here she wanders around making contact with people, stopping to chat here and there. Once a week she sets up a stall with leaflets and various guides such as welfare rights handbooks. She also has some set office hours when people can come to see her privately (3 hours). There is a fairly constant flow of people during this time - although when things are slack she can update her recordings and catch up on her 'admin'. She also has some other fairly regular pieces of project work - training for students running clubs and groups; a group for young women of colour and so on. There are also some working sessions with student union officers. The fixed spots on her planner are as in Figure 7.3. She is mainly 'around' at lunch time (shown as off-white boxes). She has two office sessions for more private work with people plus a session with the student officers ('working with - shown as grey). Lastly there are two main 'project' sessions. She then fits in other pieces of work around these.

Figure 7.3: An informal educator's planner

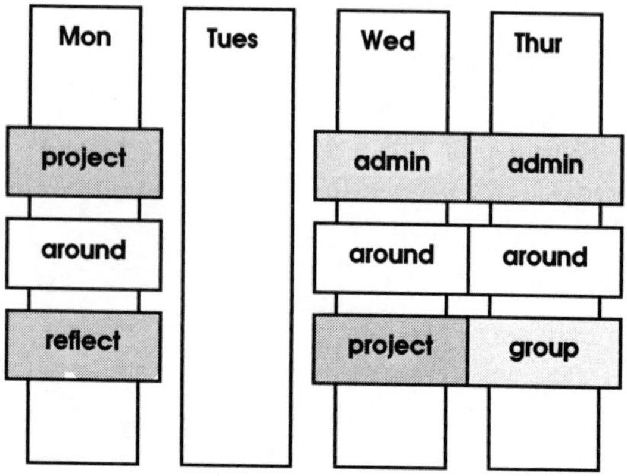

Mon	Tues	Wed	Thur	Fri
project		admin	admin	
around		around	around	
reflect		project	group	

Thinking about intensity

As we have already noted, aspects of the work involve differing degrees of depth. Sometimes we are making new contacts and maintaining relationships. Here we may simply greet people, ask how they are getting on, or talk about some TV programme or what they were doing last night. In terms of evaluating our work and reporting it to managers we can discuss this in terms of the number of contacts we make.

At other times we put on sessions or take part in activities and groups. This involves a more intense working relationship. We are looking to the processes in the group or the exchange; thinking about the subject matter; and trying to foster opportunities that can help people to gain better understandings, develop skills and to explore their values and feelings. We can think about these situations in terms of participants in sessions.

Last, there are times when we are dealing with sensitive questions - perhaps one-to-one or in a small group. We could describe this as counselling - but we prefer 'working with'. This is because we take counselling to be a specialist activity drawing heavily on psycho-dynamic insights. Educational approaches make some use of such insights but draw mainly from other, developmental, traditions. Examples here may be working with individuals around their family relationships or their strategies when dealing with social security officials. Here we may think of people as 'clients' and describe it as 'casework'. This term may indicate a long-term approach that seeks to explore how individuals can handle problem relationships and situations. [51]

From this we can see that the work of the same person may fall into different categories at various moments. To do casework we have to be known and to have contacts. The need for particular projects may emerge out of casework or from casual conversation. Each is dependent on the other. Again we are brought back to the false separation of informal and formal approaches.

Numbers

This now leads us on to the tricky question of numbers. We may complain about having to keep details of the numbers of people we work with - and of the emphasis put upon this area of work by some managers. However, there is a real point to such figures. We want to make sure that we are spending our time in the best way possible.

In thinking about numbers it is important to make some judgements about the intensity of the relationship. We make a lot of contacts, a smaller number of whom participate more intensely in groups and projects, and an even smaller number are involved as clients in casework relationships. If we then plot the amount of time involved (in this case from our student support worker) then a more complex picture emerges. We can see this in *Figure 7.4*. We may spend more time on casework (represented by the right-hand block) but have fewer 'clients'.

---

51 See Anne Masterson's (1982) *A Place of My Own*, Manchester: Greater Manchester Youth Association (also Youth Clubs UK). She explores her work as a youth worker through casework.

The $64,000 question is how many people and to what intensity should we be working in any particular setting? In answering this we have to consider, for example:

- The number of hours working time we have to play with.

- Our qualities, strengths and weaknesses as workers.

- The wishes and needs of the people we are engaging with.

- The constraints of the settings we operate in.

- The aims and policies of our agency.

Figure 7.4: Numbers and time

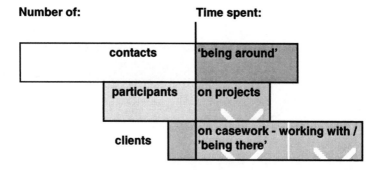

Two part-time informal educators working with young people in a small village, for example, will have a limited number of people they can work with, but it may take some time to contact them (because of physical distance). We might also expect them to place an emphasis on doing projects - partly because of the limited numbers of young people, partly because of the relative lack of local opportunities. They might organize trips, for example, or undertake various arts and cultural activities.

An informal educator with a focus on community development may spend a substantial amount of time on projects (for example, linked to various campaigns) and on the associated administration. They are also likely to devote a good deal of time to working with local groups so that they may better achieve their goals. The classic bind here is that 'being around' - knocking on doors, meeting parents at the school gate, etc. can be neglected.

Further, to make comparisons we really need to think in terms of the agency, club or unit. While a focus on individual workloads is needed when planning, questions about numbers and intensity are best approached as a whole. This allows us to properly value the contribution of workers - voluntary, part-time and full-time.

In conclusion

Several things come out from this. First, each area of work has a different shape and balance. The ease of making contact with large numbers of people within colleges and schools, and access to facilities, for example, provides informal educators in those settings with a flying start. Second, there is something of a case to combine different approaches. For example, rather than thinking of workers being attached to a particular centre or club, we should think of them being attached to an area or neighbourhood.

Many of the old distinctions, for example, between building-based and detached work; working with young people and adults; and between play work, youth work and community work, are overblown. The real questions concern the extent to which we think of ourselves as educators; our comfort in working in less overtly structured settings; and our ease in conversation.

Some questions to consider

1. Try breaking down your work under the six modes outlined here. Then work out (roughly) how much time spent on each. Do any significant patterns emerge? Are there points for action?

2. Are you around in places where the people with whom you wish to work can be found? Consider your work in relation to the patterns of life in your neighbourhood.

3. Have you made space so that you can respond to situations?

4. Think back over the last month or so. Have you paid enough attention to administration, and to exploring your practice?

Follow up

There are several things you can do to deepen your exploration of organizing the daily round.

Visit the 'organizing the daily round' support page at www.infed.org/foundations for further discussion, examples, activities and links.

Read Mark K. Smith's (1994) chapter on 'Structuring the work' in *Local Education*, Buckingham: Open University Press, pages 86-107. This provides more detail on the modes of working discussed in this chapter.

Read Paul Henderson and David N Thomas (2001) *Skills in Neighbourhood Work*, London: Routledge. The whole text is useful as guide to organising yourself, your work and organisations.

Read Ted Milburn (2001) 'Managing informal education' in Linda Deer Richardson and Mary Wolfe (eds.) (2001) *The Principles and Practice of Informal Education*, London: RoutledgeFalmer. This piece uses the model explored in this chapter.

Conclusion

F. Scott Fitzgerald's novel *The Great Gatsby* opens with the narrator Nick Carraway reflecting how, in his 'younger and vulnerable years', his father gave him some advice that he'd been turning over in his mind ever since.

> 'Whenever you feel like criticizing anyone,' he told me, 'just remember that all the people in this world haven't had the advantages that you've had.'
> He didn't say any more, but we've always been unusually communicative in a reserved way, and I understood that he meant a great deal more than that.[52]

Here is an example of how conversation lingers; endures in the memory. It can impact upon an individual's behaviour in ways and places the speaker could not foretell. In this example the father, living in the rural Mid-West, would hardly have predicted his son would fight in a European war then live in Long Island beside the mega-rich. Little did he know how poignant his words were, and would become? It is a reminder of the care we need to take around what we say. Our words may carry more weight than we envisage. What is more, volume is often less crucial than content.

Chapter One also started with an excerpt from a novel. There we noted how the character in George Eliot's book

---

[52] F Scott Fitzgerald (1974) *The Great Gatsby*, London: Penguin, page 7. First published in 1926.

visited a tavern with a purpose over and above having a drink and a convivial evening. Felix Holt mixed with people and engaged them in conversation to foster learning. He was motivated by a belief that through conversation he might contribute to changing the world. Carraway on the other hand reflected on the opinion of his father because he considered him to be a wise man. For Holt to achieve his end he had to educate himself to educate others. Carraway's father secured influence by demonstrating his wisdom via deed and word. Each reminds us that informal educators must earn the right to be heard. They must be wise and knowledgeable if they are to achieve anything worthwhile. Technique alone is never enough.

Being prepared

Increasingly formal educators are being transformed into deliverymen and women. Politicians produce compulsory curricula for them and then tell them what methods to use to 'deliver' the contents. On cue, publishers supply books and software designed to save schoolteachers having to think about how best to order or present the 'knowledge' others prioritise. Schoolteachers are then left to manage the classroom, mark exercises and ensure students do the standard tests when required. Less and less is it presumed they should know anything beyond what the students are tested upon. Indeed knowing 'too much' can make them a less efficient delivery person. It can tempt them to stray from the curriculum. Also, as others select the methods, it becomes unnecessary for schoolteachers to understand theories of learning or education. Inevitably some resist these attempts to transform their role. They may, for example, seek to create space for conversation and so engage in education rather than mere instruction. However, this can be hazardous and may sabotage their 'career prospects'.

Informal educators are not constrained to the same extent. Illiberal policymakers may want to narrow our activities by, for example, seeking to dictate with whom we work or the outcomes required, but we still have abundant opportunities for dialogue. Such autonomy creates both opportunities and problems. Here we want to highlight two.

First, for most of the time we do not work from a syllabus or curriculum that defines what should and should not be taught. This can leave us with some difficult choices. We have to decide with what and whom we want to engage. Our starting point might be that any topic raised in a genuine spirit of enquiry should be addressed provided the setting is appropriate. However, dealing with 'controversial' issues can pose problems both for other 'stakeholders', like managers and members of local communities, and for us as educators. We may be nervous about discussing, say, the case for legalising certain drugs. We cannot refuse to do so because 'we must finish the exam assignment' or 'it is an inappropriate subject for a music lesson'. Rather, we have to justify our reluctance in conversation – and that may not be easy. Dialogue and debate outside of the sanctuary of curricula can be difficult, disconcerting and even dangerous. Hurtful and unpleasant exchanges can occur, deeply held beliefs are held up to merciless scrutiny - ours as well as others. If we seek to change the world through dialogue we cannot avoid being changed ourselves.

Second, as informal educators we do not have a timetable partitioning our day neatly into subjects. We may influence conversations and promote certain topics but we cannot use sanctions if others resist. We can neither choose what is discussed or the moment at which it may arise. Indeed, we must learn to let events take their course, to fly by the seat of our pants. It is easy to see how this occurs. However, unless we attend to content, the settings we use and how we present ourselves, informal education has only very limited value. We must be ready to respond to a wide range of eventualities and be able to draw upon on a depth of experience and understanding.

Being responsive

The Parker-Gillespie set at once exploded into a duel, the weapons being trumpet and saxophone, and the common ground such established bop classics as *A*

Night in Tunisia and *Dizzy Atmosphere*. Sparks flew immediately. On the ensemble part of *Tunisia* Charlie played a fantastic counterpoint to the theme that would have routed a lesser musician than Gillespie. Off and running, Charlie plunged recklessly and breathtakingly into the alto break while Dizzy, no longer in his jolly mood, retired to gather his forces. After the break the saxophone chorus was played with a fierce, hard, professional brilliance. Dizzy came back with a chorus of equal quality, lustrous, chiselled, accurately articulated. The duel waxed its hottest on *Dizzy Atmosphere*, taken at an incredible tempo that left the drummer ... and pianist scrambling frantically. There were feints, sorties, lines paraphrased half a tone off pitch, tricky gambits, musical shorthand, stopped time, lightening excursions into strange scales and keys. Parker was the aggressor, Dizzy the counter puncher.[53]

This encounter took place in the 1950s. The two jazz musicians had not played together for a number of years and an element of rivalry had arisen. The confrontation took place during a break in a concert at which Dizzy Gillespie was the 'star billing'. Given his notorious unreliability no one was even certain Charlie Parker would appear. There had been no rehearsal but the musicians spoke a common musical language and drew upon a shared heritage.

Informal educators also work within the framework of a common language and assumptions. These can offer almost limitless opportunities for variation. By changing the inflection of our voice and manner, or the ways in which words are put together, we can alter, often subtly, what is communicated. This means we must pay special attention to what is being said. Much as musicians learn to respond to each other to create an intelligible 'performance', so informal educators must also draw out the contribution of others

---

53 R. Russell (1972) *Bird Lives! The High Life and Hard Times of Charlie 'Yardbird' Parker*, London: Quartet, pages 247-248.

whilst simultaneously making their own. After all we are seeking to stimulate, not silence, those we engage with. It is a delicate balance but one which good informal educators, like good jazz musicians, seek to maintain. Informal educators also need to react and respond sympathetically without creating disharmony. Both jazz musicians and informal educators are improvisers. They build on what goes before, develop themes and seek opportunities for creative intervention. They are both artists.

How can we prepare for this sort of encounter? What steps can we take to be able to improvise with others, to work with and survive their 'feints, sorties ... tricky gambits'? The answer is by learning our craft. We develop through constant practice, study and reflection. The musicians in our example, even those left behind, had first to command their instruments. They had to learn to play sufficiently well to engage in a musical dialogue with others. Once that level was reached, it had to be continually cultivated - otherwise they risked being sidelined. Informal educators must similarly strive to achieve greater proficiency. Words, not notes, are our currency. As a result we need a rich and varied vocabulary to understand what others are saying, share ideas and values, and maintain the interest and attention of others. Few things are more tedious than having to spend time with those whose conversation is repetitive, restricted and predictable. We need, therefore, to extend and fine-tune our communication skills. We must also rehearse by holding dialogues with others and ourselves; and read, listen to and converse with those who have important things to say. Like professional musicians we should attend the equivalent of 'Master Classes' and concerts: events where we can share in (even observe) conversations and dialogues that challenge and stretch us.

Being wise

We must also acknowledge that the capacity to use language is not enough. Glibness and a facility to entertain are rarely sufficient. As informal educators we must be educated ourselves – otherwise how might we contribute to the education of others? This means being comfortable with ideas, culturally aware and knowledgeable. As Josephine Macalister Brew put it, an informal educator should 'be capable of entertaining himself, capable of entertaining a stranger, and capable of entertaining a new idea'.[54] Wisdom lies in being able to reflect on situations, and to encourage others to join with us. It entails relating these things to the sort of practical actions that are right for a situation.[55]

A strong current of anti-intellectualism has existed within many of the settings where informal educators operate. As a result many participants are poorly served. Indifference to education remains unchallenged, even reinforced, by workers who survive on a conversational diet of gossip, chat, sport, celebrity news, soaps and the like. Cultural isolation is, thus, often sustained and sometimes encouraged by workers who themselves avoid anything challenging or profound. Too much work has entertained but not educated.

Theodore Zeldin quotes a woman he spoke to who was once a teacher and is now a local councillor and lawyer someone who, he notes, has spent much of her life talking. She told him that, 'Without conversation ... the human soul is bereft. It is almost as important as food, drink, love, exercise. It is one of the great human needs. If deprived of it, we die.'[56] Educators able to initiate and sustain such dialogue require special talents, wisdom, confidence and a rich education, in the best sense of the word.

By now some readers may well be accusing us of advocating an elitist variant of informal education. In one respect we plead guilty. We want educators willing to study, reflect upon, and perfect their craft. Those who are not competent, or for want of education can only work in a

---

[54] Josephine Macalister Brew (1946) page 28.

[55] Michele Erina Doyle and Mark K. Smith (1999) *Born and Bred. Leadership, heart and informal education*, London: Rank Foundation/YMCA George Williams College, page 25.

[56] Theodore Zeldin (1998) *Conversation: How Talk Can Change Your Life*, London: Harvill Press, page 34.

limited number of settings, pose a problem. Already there are too many people getting a second class service from second-rate practitioners. We need educators who are sophisticated and wise in their work. If such discrimination is not to continue we cannot collude with this.

Being patient

A Greek myth tells us Sisyphus betrayed the secrets of the gods to mortals. As a consequence they punished him by making him push a stone to the top of a hill. So heavy was the stone that whenever Sisyphus neared the summit he became so exhausted that it rolled down the hill and he was fated to start again. Poor Sisyphus was condemned to labour for eternity. This depressing fable might at times serve as an allegory for the 'labours of the informal educator'. Informal education unlike so many activities promises the practitioner few immediate rewards. Exams are not passed, cars are not sold, widgets are not turned out, beans are not counted. Measurable targets are not met. Informal educators working, as they do through the medium of dialogue and conversation, are rarely able to judge the impact they have, for good or ill. The extent to which we have helped others 'see things more clearly', 'decide to see it through', 'make it up with their neighbour and try to start a fresh' may never be known. Sometimes we may foster change simply by behaving in certain ways and being observed without our knowledge. Certainly as a consequence of our approach we frequently 'educate' without those we work with being aware they owe us any thanks whatsoever. Our question may have prompted their re-thinking and they solved the problem themselves. Our conscious refusal to 'do the job for them' lets them take charge.

During an interview with ex-members of a club, all now in their late 70s and 80s, one said of their ex-leader, Basil Henriques, when discussing his achievements, that she now saw his influence still at work as all their children were actively engaged in community and charity work. The six ex-members then recounted an astounding array of middle-aged people enthusiastically engaged in voluntary club, charity, social and community work. Basil Henriques' inspirational dedication to the service of others and the wider community, expressed in his club work, they told one us, had a produced a legacy that simply could not be measured[57]. These and others all recounted verbatim, conversations that they had had with Henriques and other club workers that they firmly believed had significantly influenced their lives. These were conversations that the other party probably had not invested with a great deal of consequence.

Evaluation forms handed out at the end of a session and tick boxes completed tell us nothing concerning the value of what might have been achieved. Not least because change often takes time, learning is cumulative and meaningful dialogue usually demands reflection over time. Informal educators must have patience. They have to accept that they are playing a long game. Also, they must have faith in the worth of the work they undertake.

Let us return briefly to poor Sisyphus. The French philosopher Albert Camus wrote an essay on the story. In it he suggests that we must always consciously seek to choose a way of living that is worth living. Camus argues even the pitiful Sisyphus can do this. For, 'There is no fate that cannot be surmounted by scorn …. The struggle itself toward the heights is enough to fill a man's heart. One must imagine Sisyphus happy.[58] Patience towards our work and faith in it's worth and value will us be 'happy', sometimes against all the odds.

---

[57] For a more extensive account of the work of Henriques that draws on these and other interviews see Tony Jeffs (2004) 'Basil Henriques and the "House of Friendship"' in Ruth Gilchrist, Tony Jeffs and Jean Spence (eds.) *Architects of Change: Studies in the History of Community and Youth Work.* Leicester: Youth Work Press.

[58] Albert Camus (1969) *The Myth of Sisyphus and Other Essays.* New York: Alfred Knopf page 123.

In conclusion

Conversation can bring people together, confront individuals and groups with ideas, challenge their preconceptions and nourish the craving for a better world. It can address barriers of class, 'race' and gender, but it can also reaffirm divisions. Informal educators can make a difference, but we need to face some important issues.

First, there is always the danger, to paraphrase Tawney, of dwelling on the problem of poverty and never getting around to tackling the problem of greed. Targeting resources only at those who are socially excluded can all too easily confirm their position rather than improve it. When those resources include workers who lack the ability to engage, educate and challenge, the situation is worsened. Without changing the way we all think, those who are poor, marginalized and disadvantaged are likely to be disregarded by the rest. Equally, those labelled as 'privileged' can remain trapped and diminished in their own worldview. Transformatory education looks to both the oppressed and the oppressor.

Second, education that seeks to foster democracy and vision is inherently risky. Educators and policymakers alike tend to shy away from it. It is difficult, unpredictable and does not offer the desired level of control. But vision is not created through the dull routines of a national curriculum or the safety of the formal environment.[59] To grow and develop, people need the freedom to experience the world, to make mistakes, and to challenge the taken-for-granted. They need to be able to engage with each other.

Third, a concern for democracy and learning from life as it is lived requires some basic changes in the way we view education. Schools need to be radically reshaped; the obsession in education generally with targets, qualifications and economic utility diminished; and the attention of educators focused less on individual achievement and more on relationships and people-in-association. It will take a lot

---

[59] Charles Handy (1999) *The New Alchemists*, London: Hutchinson.

to unsettle the mix of vested interest, lack of vision and poverty of understanding that currently characterizes educational debate and policymaking in the UK and many other countries. However, this should not stop us from trying. Spaces for conversation and commitment can be created. Addressing the flaws in our own thinking and practice can open up considerable possibility. And last, but not least, we need to have faith in education. Exploring democracy, conversation and learning with others will bear fruit if there is truth in what we say.

We began by stressing the challenge of informal education. It, thus, seems fitting that we conclude by highlighting, but not dwelling on, some of the challenges that face informal educators. First is the growing pressure to 'deliver' outcomes that can be measured in terms of boxes ticked 'satisfied' or products such as reduced offending rates in a given district. Informal educators have always set themselves rigorous targets. For example - they have always sought to reduce violent behaviour, not encourage it; stimulate autonomy not promote dependency; advance the well-being of individuals and communities not the deterioration. These are big outcomes that can only be achieved over many years of sustained work. The problem with having to focus on the 'delivery' of the immediate variety is that they force the workers to put on the back-burner the important longer term issues and to neglect those members of the community who will not deliver a measurable outcome.

Second, and closely related to the first, is the increasing use of funding that is both short-term and tied to particular forms of activity or client groups. This works against reflective practice that builds upon the needs of those we work with. It also, as it is intended to do, seriously erodes the autonomy of the work. It changes us from educators to the deliverers of pre-packed 'modules' and training packs. Eventually it trivialises the work and places outside the agenda the difficult and challenging 'big issues'. These are issues that politicians and managers find themselves uncomfortable with, for example - impending environmental collapse, the threat of growing religious intolerance and conflict, corporate crime and abuse, exploitation of cheap labour. Unless we, as workers, are willing to debate and enter into dialogue about the macro and as well as the micro issues then we will eventually neuter ourselves.

The issues we have briefly discussed are deep-seated and profound; they perpetually test our commitment and courage. They also make the work worthwhile and offer continuous opportunities for us to grow.

Follow up

Visit the support page at www.infed.org/foundations for further discussion and links.

Read Josephine Macalister Brew's (1946) 'The approach to informal education' in *Informal Education. Adventures and reflections*, London: Faber and Faber, pages 29-46. Brew's was the first full-length text on informal education – and the themes and approaches she identifies can still help us to think about the shape of practice. You can find articles by Brew and an appreciation of her work via the support page.

Read Tony Jeffs and Mark K Smith (1990) *Using Informal Education*, Buckingham: Open University Press. This is a collection of essays including eight by practitioners who look at aspects of their work in detail. The first chapter 'Using Informal Education' and last 'Educating Informal Educators' by the editors provide useful accounts of some of the key debates. Available via the support page.

Read Theodore Zeldin (1998) *Conversation: How Talk Can Change Your Life*, London: Harvill Press. A short and somewhat quirky book that, nevertheless, manages to convey some of the trials and excitement of engaging in conversation, whether for pleasure, self-education or work. It is not an academic book, although written by an academic, but the text of a series of six talks broadcast by Radio Four.

A note on terms

Many who work as informal educators do not always describe themselves as such. They may opt for labels that reflect their 'client group' or where they work. For this reason we examine some of the terms that may be used to describe the work. More detailed discussion of these terms can be found in *the encyclopaedia of informal education*: www.infed.org.

Lifelong learning

Lifelong learning has become something of a catchphrase in UK policy debates in recent years. A common sense starting point would be that it refers to the distribution of learning throughout a person's lifespan. It would, thus, include the learning associated with involvement in family life, formal education, clubs and groups, and work. However, in current policy usage it tends to refer to the learning of adults and is often associated with the development of skills for economic success. In this responsibility for developing learning opportunities for adults is increasingly seen as less a matter for the state than for individuals and employers. While there is talk of informal learning and informal education it is often poorly theorized and seen as something to 'progress' from.

Community education and community learning

Community educators in Scotland and in many Southern countries have similar concerns and approaches as 'informal educators'. For us the main distinction lays in the ways that workers view the setting in which they operate. Community educators may see themselves as educating *for* community, *in* the community. Informal educators may also be working to further democracy and commitment to others, but they may not label the setting for their activities as being 'in the community'. A social worker in a residential home may see it as *a* community, but not as *the* community as a whole.

In Scotland there has been a shift in recent years away from community education into the idea of cultivating community learning - 'informal learning and social development work with individuals and groups in their communities. The aim of this work is to strengthen communities by improving people's knowledge, skills and confidence, organisational ability and resources'.[60]

Non-formal education

Some may describe part of our focus as non-formal education. In this view, informal education is the lifelong process in which people learn from everyday experience; and non-formal education is organized educational activity outside formal systems[61]. The distinction made is largely administrative. Formal education is linked with schools and training institutions; non-formal with community groups and other organizations; and informal covers what is left, e.g. interactions with friends, family and work colleagues. The problem here is that people often organize educational events as part of their everyday experience and so the lines

---

[60] Scottish Executive (2003) *Working and learning together to build stronger communities. Working draft Community Learning and Development Guidance, Edinburgh*: Scottish Executive. Available via the support page.

[61] P. H. Coombs and M. Ahmed (1974) *Attacking Rural Poverty. How non-formal education can help*, Baltimore: John Hopkins University Press. We discuss the problems with this in (1990) *Using Informal Education*, Buckingham: Open University Press.

blur rapidly. We focus on informal and formal education to bring out issues around setting, aim and process.

Popular education

The meaning of this term has changed over time and differs according to the political and cultural context. Today the most common understanding derives from practice in a number of South America countries. It generally implies the following characteristics:

1. The educational experience is progressive in orientation and content, and designed to produce social and political change (to the benefit of the oppressed and least well-off).

2. The content relates to concrete experience and interests of those engaged in political struggles.

3. The pedagogical approach is collective in orientation. Group rather than individual learning is the focus.

4. Practice seeks to link education at all levels with social movements seeking progressive social change.[62]

Social pedagogy and social education

In Germany our focus here may be described as social pedagogy and associated with social work and, perhaps, a 'problem-focus'. It is a perspective, 'including social action which aims to promote human welfare through child-rearing and education practices; and to prevent or ease social problems by providing people with the means to manage their own lives, and make changes in their circumstances'[63].

---

[62] See Jim Crowther, Ian Martin and Mae Shaw (1999) *Popular Education and Social Movements in Scotland Today*, Leicester: NIACE, for an exploration of how popular education might relate to a northern context.

[63] Crescy Cannan, Lynne Berry and Karen Lyons (1992) *Social Work in Europe*, London: Macmillan, pages 73-4.

Originally, in the mid 1800s, the term was used for a way of thinking about schooling as education *for* community (or sociality). Hence, social pedagogy is sometimes translated as 'community education'. In North America it was talked of as 'social education' - and connected with many of John Dewey's (and our) concerns. In Britain social education has tended to be used rather more to describe the process of fostering personal development and achieving maturity. It has a more individualistic orientation and may not put 'sharing in a common life' at its core, although there has been an emphasis on working with groups. More recently in England the notion of social pedagogy has been used to describe the activities of child care, play and youth workers within children's trusts.

Youth work and community work

Some youth workers and community workers describe themselves as educators. Others may view themselves, first and foremost, as organizers (of groups and activities), or as case or care workers. As a result, youth work and community work can take very different forms. To limit confusion we focus on aim and 'client group':

- **Youth work**: work with young people that is committed to furthering their happiness and well-being.

- **Community work**: work that fosters peoples' commitment to their neighbours; and participation in, and development of, local, democratic forms of organization.

If we think about these as educational processes, then much of what is claimed to be special about them relates to qualities associated with informal education. Examples include the concern with conversation, reflection on experience, choice, and participation. In other words, if workers see themselves as educators then their work can be best approached as informal education either with young people or with people in particular communities.

Index